Edwin M. Schur is Professor and Chairman of the Department of Sociology at Tufts University. He is the author of *Narcotic Addiction in Britain and America: The Impact of Public Policy* and editor of *The Family and the Sexual Revolution.* Dr. Schur is a graduate of the London School of Economics, where he received his Ph.D. in Sociology, and of Yale Law School, and has been admitted to the Connecticut Bar. He is an associate editor of the *American Sociological Review.*

CRIMES WITHOUT VICTIMS

Deviant Behavior and Public Policy

ABORTION
HOMOSEXUALITY
DRUG ADDICTION

Edwin M. Schur

Prentice-Hall, Inc. A SPECTRUM BOOK *Englewood Cliffs, N.J.*

Current printing (last digit):

12

© 1965 BY PRENTICE-HALL, INC.

ENGLEWOOD CLIFFS, NEW JERSEY

LIBRARY OF CONGRESS CATALOG NO.: 65-12304

Printed in the United States of America—C. P 19293, C 19294

PREFACE

The three types of deviance discussed in this book lie at the borderline of crime. There has long been dispute as to whether they should be considered crimes, sins, vices, diseases, or simply as patterns of social deviance. In each case the offending behavior involves a willing and private exchange of strongly demanded yet officially proscribed goods and services; this element of consent precludes the existence of a victim—in the usual sense of the word. Each of these problems also has certain medical—as well as legal, psychological, and sociological—aspects. Although this complexity has fostered useful research and analysis by specialists in various fields, it has also produced a somewhat confusing range of views as to the methods with which such behavior should be dealt. To the extent that sociologists have studied these borderline problems at all, their goal of detached scientific observation (of "ethical neutrality") has inhibited whatever interest they might feel in directly challenging substantive criminal law provisions. Yet, as this volume tries to suggest, key aspects of the problem being studied may be directly or indirectly attributable to such legal proscriptions. Policy is not merely a reaction to an existing problem; rather, the relation between policy and problem is reciprocal. A specific policy may cause new problems, or make existing ones worse, and the sociologist must take this into account.

It is partly to illustrate this interrelation of problem and policy that three "crimes without victims" are discussed here. The discussion should have the further value of focusing on some topics which have been largely neglected by sociologists. The social problems of abortion and homosexuality are almost completely by-passed in existing texts; drug addiction often is discussed, but in such instances the role of policy is usually considered only as an afterthought. It is hoped that the present study will prove useful in supplementing conventional textbooks in criminology, deviance, and social problems, and be of interest to the general reader.

Although this volume deals with some basic questions I have been working on for a number of years, the actual manuscript was prepared while I was on a year's leave of absence from Tufts University, and in residence at the Center for the Study of Law and Society, University of California, Berkeley. I am grateful to the Russell Sage Foundation and to Tufts for making that opportunity possible. Throughout the course of this work I have benefited especially from extensive discussion with, and critical comment on early draft materials by, Sheldon L. Messinger and David Matza

At various stages I have also received helpful criticisms and suggestions from the following persons: Jerome E. Carlin, Lewis A. Coser, H. Laurence Ross, Jerome H. Skolnick, Neil Smelser, and Albert D. Ullman. I should like to thank Mary Ann Gisondi, Peter Grenquist, and James M. Murray of Prentice-Hall, Inc. for their many helpful suggestions and careful attention to the manuscript, and Joan Smith and Lois Karp for their diligent work in typing it.

E. M. S.

CONTENTS

Contents

Deviance and Public Policy

The "Creation" of Deviance

In the study of deviant behavior and crime, much more attention has been focused on the deviating individuals than on the social "definitions" of the deviance. Yet, as Howard S. Becker has pointed out:

> Deviance is *not* a quality of the act the person commits, but rather a consequence of the application by others of rules and sanctions to an "offender." The deviant is one to whom that label has successfully been applied; deviant behavior is behavior that people so label.[1]

When definitions of deviance take the specific form of criminal laws, the sociologist may be particularly likely to neglect their bearing on the behavior in question. Understandably, sociologists are somewhat less interested in law than lawyers are. Furthermore, there has been a general tendency for sociologists to focus greater attention on informal mechanisms of social control. In many instances, however, no real sociological understanding of the deviance problem being considered is possible unless the role of legal norms is examined. This is not to suggest that the sociologist need engage himself in detailed or technical legal analysis; rather, he must consider the important ways in which specific legal definitions and law enforcement policies influence the development of such problems.

Sociology has expanded the analysis of deviance well beyond the narrow individual-centered (even body-centered) schemes that once prevailed. Attempts to relate deviance to the general social struc-

1

ture have helped to balance the treatment (even by some sociologists) of deviant and criminal acts as though they were aberrations rather than integral elements of social life. Yet the particular forms of deviance are frequently ignored. They are considered mere symptoms of underlying social strains and disruptions—in a way that may reveal the impact of psychological theories in this area. And the researcher or analyst is likely to be more concerned with developing a theory of deviance than with understanding any specific form of deviant behavior. This has been evident in the tendency to seek research populations of "criminals" or "delinquents" (as such), with little concern for the varying categories of behavior subsumed under such a rubric. Certainly it is natural for sociologists, in their search for generalizations, to seek out the common elements in diverse behavior patterns and processes. At the same time, however, the search for correlates of deviance should not be allowed to obscure other related sociological concerns. Thus, the *very existence* of a particular deviant behavior pattern in a society is an important datum for research, as is the nature of the social reaction to that behavior and the interplay between the two.

The concept of deviance has itself exerted a helpful influence—especially in underlining the point that deviance can be fully understood only in relation to conformity. On the other hand, it would be most unfortunate if it inadvertently served to perpetuate the preoccupation with deviating individuals.[2] A difficulty has been that in those social problem areas in which deviant or offending individuals are reasonably identifiable, research has concentrated on the question of cause, narrowly construed. It has been the compelling concern, for example, to determine *why* some individuals turn to crime though others do not. When attention is almost exclusively focused on the underlying forces pushing individuals into deviance, there is relatively little consideration of just *what* the deviance itself is. Indeed, various specific forms of deviance are often viewed as being caused by the same underlying forces.

Deviance as a Process

The notion of deviance as a social process suggests an alternative approach. This concept reflects the basic recognition that deviant behavior, like other forms of social behavior, is learned through social interaction. This is not a new idea, even if it is now being given new emphasis by one group of sociologists. A classic statement of the view, as it has developed in the study of crime, was made by Frank Tannenbaum:

> No more self-defeating device could be discovered than the one society has developed in dealing with the criminal. It proclaims his career in such loud and dramatic forms that both he and the community accept the judgment as a fixed description. He becomes conscious of himself as a criminal, and the community expects him to live up to his reputation, and will not credit him if he does not live up to it.[3]

A central thesis in this kind of analysis is that self-fulfilling-prophecy mechanisms[4] help to explain deviance.

One of the most systematic efforts to elucidate a theory of deviance in interactional or processual terms has been made by Edwin Lemert. A key feature of his analysis is the recognition that deviance cannot be understood without reference to the societal reactions it invokes. Viewing deviance as but one aspect of social differentiation, Lemert goes on to examine the interplay between the deviant and his judges, highlighting the significant ways in which the deviance comes to be shaped by the attitudes and actions of others. He particularly notes the impact of societal reactions on the organization of deviants, and also draws a highly important distinction between primary and secondary deviation:

> When a person begins to employ his deviant behavior or a role based upon it as a means of defense, attack, or adjustment to the overt and covert problems created by the consequent societal reaction to him, his deviation is secondary.[5]

A valuable elaboration of this approach—as seen in recent writings of Erving Goffman and Howard Becker—has involved the application of the "career" concept to deviant behavior. The idea of a criminal career—to describe the actions of professional and habitual offenders—is not new. But there is a broader sense in which every deviant has a "career." This is not simply a sequence of discrete events in the individual's life history; it is the subtle and continuous interplay that Goffman describes as a person's "moral career"—"the regular sequence of changes that career entails in the person's self and in his framework of imagery for judging himself and others." [6]

Also highly useful in this regard is the concept of "career contingencies." Just as it can be said that mental patients "distinctively suffer not from mental illness, but from contingencies," [7] deviants, too, may be generally viewed as displaying contingencies. The actions of others have crucially shaped the deviant outcome. This fact has been recognized by sociologists, who are now increasingly turning their attention to the administration of criminal justice and the intricacies of correctional organizations and techniques.

Important emphasis has been placed on the impact on the individual of being caught, labeled, and publicly "processed" as a deviant. And, as Becker has stated: "Whether a person takes this step [or steps] depends not so much on what he does as on what other people do, on whether or not they enforce the rule he has violated." [8]

The societal reaction to the deviant, then, is vital to an understanding of the deviance itself and a major element in—if not a cause of—the deviant behavior. A related point of some significance, long realized by sociologists, is that the definition of some behavior as "deviant" serves positive functions for the conformists, enhancing group cohesion and strengthening the sense of group membership among such individuals.[9] An appreciation of these functions is also necessary for a complete explanation of deviance.

In his perceptive study, *Stigma*,[10] Erving Goffman discusses some problems of identity and of interpersonal relations which face many stigmatized individuals. For purposes of that analysis, the fact of stigmatization is assumed as a point of departure. Certain personal characteristics are such, of course, that other people can very easily use them as bases for social stigmatization. Highly visible physical handicaps and disfigurements, and membership in a minority racial group, fall into this category. Because of the crucial relevance of sex to questions of personal identity, confirmed homosexuality (if recognized) seems also to carry a built-in stigma. But not all kinds of "differentness" or deviating behavior are equally stigmatizable, nor is being easily stigmatizable the same as actually being stigmatized. In any case, as Goffman himself rightly notes, "the perceived undesirability of a *particular* personal property, and its capacity to trigger off these stigma-normal processes, has a history of its own, a history that is regularly changed by purposeful social action." [11]

The Criminalization of Deviance

The definition of behavior as "criminal" is an extreme form of stigmatization. Defining behavior as "deviant" has profound effects on those individuals engaging in it; what might be termed *the criminalization of deviance* pushes the process one step further. As already indicated, public branding as the perpetrator of a specific "criminal" act is a crucial step in the individual's progress toward a criminal "career." Criminal conviction—perhaps even mere prosecution—may automatically and retrospectively effect crucial modifications in a person's identity. Criminal proceedings are, in Harold Garfinkel's phrase, status-degradation ceremonies:

> The work of the denunciation effects the recasting of the objective character of the perceived other: The other person becomes in the eyes of his condemners literally a different and new person . . . the former identity stands as accidental; the new identity is the "basic reality." What he is now is what, "after all," he was all along.[12]

But the impact on the deviant of this criminalization of his behavior transcends any actual experience of official reaction. Even when he is not publicly identified and officially dealt with, he is only too aware that his behavior is legally proscribed as well as socially disapproved. Sensing that he is different or is doing an unusual act is one thing; feeling that his act is strongly disapproved is another; and knowledge that he has become a lawbreaker yet another.

Just as the mere knowledge that he has become a "criminal" may alter the individual's self-image, so too may legal proscription drive him into various behavior patterns that reinforce this image and that create new problems for himself and for society at large. As will be seen in the specific examples that follow, the formation of deviant subcultures, as well as the occurrence of certain types of secondary deviation (including secondary crime), may be crucially related to the criminalization of particular forms of socially disapproved behavior. And beyond the significant impact on particular deviating individuals, criminalization may also produce broader alterations of a deviant behavior situation—as when it establishes the economic basis for black-market operations or helps to produce situations in which police efficiency is impaired and police corruption encouraged. With respect to these latter points, the direct influence of the law may be fairly clear. On the other hand, the influence of criminalization on the self-image, the secondary deviance, and the subcultural involvement of the offender are more elusive. It is, after all, extremely difficult to separate (even for purposes of analysis) the influence of the law itself from that of the social disapproval inevitably accompanying it. Only rarely is it possible to make a partially controlled comparative analysis—for example, of the behavior and outlooks of a particular class of deviants in a jurisdiction where social and legal proscription prevail with those of the same class of deviants in a comparable jurisdiction in which there is only social disapproval of the deviance in question. In the discussion of three specific deviance problems, it will be seen that there is some such comparative evidence available. But such data do not provide a basis for concluding that particular effects stem definitely or exclusively from the law. At the same time, it would be foolish to believe that the fact of legal proscription is meaningless. Much of what is said in this book about the effects of law is meant to be primarily suggestive in nature—to show how criminal law provisions may influence particular deviance situations, to mention data already available which throw some light on this question, and to suggest some key points which require further research.

Sociologists have, perhaps, been too much impressed by the fact that criminal laws do not always effectively curb the behavior they proscribe. One must be on guard against assuming that, because a law does not prevent certain acts from occurring, it is therefore without effect. The instances examined in this book all involve laws which are highly ineffective from the standpoint of sheer deterrence, yet they may have pronounced impact—through their influence on the social meanings read into various acts or behavior patterns, and through their role in structuring total problem situations. Indeed, it is precisely the criminal laws which fail to deter which may be of greatest interest to the sociologist. In a sense, no existing criminal law ever fully achieves its stated goals. As Sutherland pointed out:

> Laws have accumulated because the mores have been weak and inconsistent; and because the laws have not had the support of the mores they have been relatively ineffective as a means of control. When the mores are adequate laws are unnecessary; when the mores are inadequate, the laws are ineffective.[13]

But some criminal laws are a good deal less enforceable than others. Unenforceable criminal law serves as an indicator of inconsistencies in a society's value system; it may reveal conflicts of interest (both economic and more general) underlying the legal structure and may serve to pinpoint significant loci of social change.

Latent Functions

The persistence of manifestly unworkable criminal laws provides an interesting illustration of the key role which latent functions[14] may play in underpinning legally institutionalized norms. Such latent functions of unenforceable laws represent really just another facet of the functions of crime. As already noted, crime or other deviance promotes solidarity in the group. It may serve psychological functions for conforming individuals and, may also serve quite definite economic functions which may—in turn—give rise to a variety of vested interests in its continuation (on the part of specialized law enforcement agencies, for example, as well as on the part of professionalized offenders). As Willard Waller pointed out some years ago: "Social problems are not solved because people do not want to solve them. . . . Solving social problems would necessitate a change in the organizational mores from which they arise." [15] This realization should strengthen the conviction that problems of deviance are rooted in a great deal more than the characteristics of deviating individuals. Such considerations suggest also the value of attempting to bring the legal reaction into the sociological analysis of deviance. In studies of this sort, the basic unit of analysis should be what may be called a "specific deviance complex." *Specific,* because more attention must be paid to particular types of offending behavior; *complex,* because neither the behavior itself nor the legal norm-and-process is to be considered separately. Rather, the entire sociolegal problem situation must be viewed as a complex of interrelated elements. As the Preface emphasizes, the relation between deviance and public policy is reciprocal.

Perhaps because of their special interest in offenders, as distinguished from offenses, criminologists have focused mainly on major crimes—violent crimes against persons and serious crimes against property. As a result, they have been dealing primarily with those criminal laws which are in fact relatively well enforced. Probably the main exception has been white-collar crime, which has interested sociologists precisely because it raises some of the general points mentioned above.[16]

The three types of deviance examined in this book illustrate a type of unenforceable law that has also created some special interest, on the part of criminal law specialists as well as sociologists. The attempt to control, by criminal law, the willing exchange of socially disapproved but widely demanded goods or services seems particularly likely to create secondary deviance and to set the stage for police corruption and demoralization. There will be occasion, in the concluding chapter, to consider whether this category of crimes without victims does really constitute a meaningful sociological entity, or whether such cases simply illustrate the more general problem of criminal laws on which public consensus is lacking. At the very least, however, the three problems focused on in this volume are interesting and challenging examples of unenforceable law.

Sociologists and the Law

So far it has been suggested only that the provisions of the substantive criminal law should be of interest in the sociological analysis of certain types of deviant behavior. There is the further possibility, however, that sociologists may have a direct interest in contributing to the formulation of such law. One legal expert has stated: "The question, what sorts of behavior should be declared criminal, is one to which the behavioral sciences might contribute vital insights. This they have largely failed to do, and we are the poorer for it." [17] Sociological inattention to this task derives largely from the recognition that law is part of the normative realm, that legal formulations and decisions invariably involve making basic value choices. Because the sociologist knows he cannot "prove" values, he may conclude that he is unable to answer the basic questions posed in legal issues and that therefore any contribution to legal policy-making falls outside the proper scope of his professional activities. This argument can be turned around, however. Because a value choice must always be made, and because there can never be any scientific proof of the "right" choice (by the sociologist or by anybody else), should not the sociologist feel fully justified in offering any evidence he can provide which will help establish a sound basis for policy decisions?

Another problem is posed by the fact that typically the lawmaker must decide *now*, whereas the scientist may be unwilling to advise until all the evidence is in. Actually, of course, all the evidence will never be in; it is the very nature of scientific findings that they are provisional. At the same time, policy is continuous, and if the sociologist withholds whatever contribution he could make, he may in a sense implicitly lend support to existing laws. As the analyses that follow make clear, it is quite true that the sociologist can never prove what the "proper" or "best" policy in any problem area might be. Yet broadly based sociological analysis of a deviance problem can throw considerable light on the evident or likely consequences of alternative legal policies. Thus policy considerations as well as sociological questions should direct the sociologist's attention to the substantive criminal law as a key aspect of problems of deviance.

Notes

[1] Howard S. Becker, *Outsiders: Studies in the Sociology of Deviance* (New York: The Free Press of Glencoe, Inc., 1963), p. 9. See also Kai Erickson, "Notes on the Sociology of Deviance," *Social Problems,* 9 (Spring 1962), 307-14; and John Kitsuse, "Societal Reaction to Deviant Behavior," *Social Problems,* 9 (Winter 1962), 247-56.

[2] See Edwin M. Schur, "Recent Social Problems Texts: An Essay-Review," *Social Problems,* 10 (Winter 1963), 287-92.

[3] Frank Tannenbaum, *Crime and the Community* (New York: Ginn & Company, 1938), p. 477.

[4] Robert K. Merton, *Social Theory and Social Structure,* rev. ed. (New York: The Free Press of Glencoe, Inc., 1957), pp. 421-36.

[5] Edwin Lemert, *Social Pathology* (New York: McGraw-Hill Book Company, Inc., 1951), p. 75.

[6] Erving Goffman, "The Moral Career of the Mental Patient," in *Asylums* (New York: Doubleday & Company, Inc., 1961), p. 128.

[7] *Ibid.,* p. 135.

[8] Becker, *op. cit.,* p. 31.

[9] Emile Durkheim, *Division of Labor in Society,* translated by G. Simpson (New York: The Free Press of Glencoe, Inc., 1960), pp. 96-110; alsco see Erickson, *op. cit.,* and Lewis A. Coser, "Some Functions of Deviance and Normative Flexibility," *American Journal of Sociology,* 68 (September 1962), 172-81.

[10] Erving Goffman, *Stigma: Notes on the Management of Spoiled Identity* (Englewood Cliffs, N.J.: Prentice-Hall, Inc., 1963).

[11] *Ibid.,* p. 138.

[12] Harold Garfinkel, "Conditions of Successful Degradation Ceremonies," *American Journal of Sociology,* 61 (March 1956), 421-22.

[13] Edwin Sutherland and Donald Cressey, *Principles of Criminology,* 6th ed. (Philadelphia: J. B. Lippincott Co., 1960), p. 11.

[14] See Merton, *op. cit.,* pp. 19-84.

[15] Willard Waller, "Sociology and the Mores," *American Sociological Review,* 1 (December 1936), 928.

[16] Vilhelm Aubert, "White-Collar Crime and Social Structure," *American Journal of Sociology,* 58 (November 1952), 263-71.

[17] Francis Allen, "Criminal Justice, Legal Values and the Rehabilitative Ideal," *Journal of Criminal Law, Criminology and Police Science,* 50 (September-October 1959). 228.

ABORTION

Abortion is the termination of pregnancy before the unborn child or fetus attains viability—i.e., capacity for life outside the womb. In this discussion the term *abortion* refers only to induced or intentional abortion; it does not include miscarriage, which is technically designated *spontaneous abortion*.

According to an authoritative anthropological survey, it appears that abortion is a universal phenomenon, and that "it is impossible even to construct an imaginary social system in which no woman would ever feel at least impelled to abort." [1] There have always been women who became pregnant against their wills, and different cultures have chosen different ways of dealing with this problem. Abortion has been incurred for almost every conceivable reason, and through a vast array of techniques. Cross-cultural evidence also reveals tremendous variation in the acceptable grounds for abortion.

In the United States, legal norms regarding abortion are highly restrictive. A well-publicized illustration of this fact was provided in 1962 by the case of Mrs. Robert Finkbine, a thirty-year-old resident of Arizona and the mother of four children. Early in her pregnancy, Mrs. Finkbine had taken some tranquilizers containing thalidomide—a drug later revealed to lead to a high rate of birth deformities when taken by pregnant women. Believing that the birth of a deformed baby would impose an undue hardship on the other members of the family, Mrs. Finkbine and her husband sought medical advice. Although at first reluctant to have an abortion, they eventually decided that such a step would be best for all concerned. A panel of staff physicians at a local hospital agreed that the operation should be performed, and this decision was concurred in by examining psychiatrists. At the last minute, however, the doctors

11

were overruled by the hospital administrator, who demanded clarification of the operation's legal status. Mrs. Finkbine then sought
from the Arizona courts a declaratory judgment certifying that her
abortion would fall within the statutory exception ("when necessary
to preserve the mother's life"). She was unable to obtain it. As a
result of this setback, Mrs. Finkbine decided "to seek help in a
more favorable legal climate," and eventually obtained a legal abortion in Sweden, where the laws on this matter are much less restrictive.[2] Although the Finkbine case generated great public concern
regarding adequate testing of drugs prior to their release on the
open market, it led to surprisingly little pressure for the reform of
American abortion laws. Apparently there was but slight dismay
that a respectable mother of four should be required to go to another country to obtain socially and legally sanctioned medical help.

Although Mrs. Finkbine's specific problem was an unusual one,
there is nothing very unusual about the demand for, and the obtaining of, abortions in this country. Summing up extensive research
on a sample of over 5000 white nonprison females, the late Dr. Alfred Kinsey reported that, by the time they were forty-five years of
age, 22 per cent of the married women had had one or more induced
abortions.[3] According to careful evaluation by an expert statistical
committee established by the Planned Parenthood Federation's 1955
conference on abortion, the number of induced abortions in the
United States each year is probably at least 200,000, and may be as
high as 1.2 million.[4] Available evidence indicates that the women
seeking abortions are of all races, religions, and socioeconomic
classes; many are married, and often already mothers. Under the
laws of the various American states—which generally permit abortion only when medically necessary to save the mother's life—most
of these abortions are illegal.

Because inducing abortion does usually contravene existing legal
norms, it may be considered a form of deviant behavior. Yet abortion often is undertaken to prevent serious family disorganization
and economic hardship or to cope with major threats to the pregnant woman's physical or psychological health. Thus although its
legal status as deviance may be established, abortion must also be
viewed as a mechanism of social control.[5] (Perhaps this merely illustrates the broader contention that definitions of deviance always

tend to be relative and that deviance is not primarily a quality of particular acts but rather a way of describing rules about which there is always disagreement.)

Therapeutic Abortion

The intentional termination of pregnancy for reasons of medical necessity is called a *therapeutic abortion*. Though a few states allow interruption of pregnancy on fairly broad medical grounds—"to preserve the mother's life or health," or "to secure the safety of the mother"—most prohibit abortion except when it is necessary to preserve the life of the mother.[6] It would seem that medical practitioners should be the ones to determine when an operation is therapeutic and when it is not. Yet the doctor's freedom to make such determinations is severely restricted by the narrow statutory definition of this term. As will become clear, the phrase *necessary to preserve the life of the mother* has little relevance to most applications for medical abortion today. Furthermore, many leading obstetricians would favor the granting of abortions under conditions not now recognized by the law. As one recent legal analysis noted, if one defines as "therapeutic" those abortions regularly performed by licensed physicians in the course of their medical practice, one must still ask to what extent these operations are (strictly speaking) legal. On the basis of a survey of 29 California hospitals, this study concluded that "many routinely performed therapeutic abortions fall outside any possible statement of the legal justification, while more are at best of dubious legality." [7]

Not only are reputable doctors and hospitals breaking the law, but at the same time hospitals are severely constrained by the statutory requirements; hence very few abortions are now performed in hospitals. The laws restricting such operations are modeled essentially after an English law of 1803—and have undergone little change despite the tremendous medical advances and social changes since that time. It is worth emphasizing at the outset that concern about medical complications is definitely not the major reason for unwillingness to perform hospital abortions. The real dangers of the clandestine operation, crudely performed by an untrained person, have tended to obscure the relative safety of a careful abortion operation. The usual hospital procedure is dilatation and curetage: the physician dilates the cervix, introduces a curette (a long, semi-sharp spoon-like instrument), and scrapes the uterine cavity. Although this technique must be restricted to the first few months of pregnancy, during that period it is quick, simple, and quite harmless. An acknowledged expert has stated:

> There is little scientific evidence that in the United States today
> . . . any marked deterioration in the physical condition of women,
> aborted for therapeutic reasons in a hospital setting, will take place.
> . . . If the operation is properly performed so that no infection or
> laceration of the cervix results, it will have no effect on either the
> health of the woman or her reproductive future.[8]

In recent years there has been a pronounced decline in the rate of therapeutic abortions. For example, a report on such operations noted that in New York the rate of such abortions per 1000 live births had fallen from 5.1 in 1943 to 2.9 in 1953 (a decline of 43 per cent). Similarly, the rate per 1000 deliveries at Los Angeles County Hospital fell from 9.4 during 1931-35 to 0.3 by 1946-50.[9] Recent statistics on 26 California hospitals show a rate of one therapeutic abortion for every 386 deliveries in 1952, dropping to one for every 431 in 1956 (with a total of 115 therapeutic abortions for the 26 hospitals during that year.)[10] Figures show an over-all decline in hospital abortions in other localities as well. Both early and recent studies also reveal considerable variation in the rates of therapeutic abortions for particular hospitals, even within the same city.

The general decline in hospital abortions is largely the result of medical advances in the treatment of conditions that once constituted major threats to pregnancy. Women with heart disease, hypertensive renal disease, tuberculosis, and other serious conditions are increasingly allowed to fulfill the term of pregnancy. Severe vomiting was once considered an indication for abortion; today this is rarely the case. Of course, a very serious medical condition may still call for abortion. Yet increased medical knowledge and improved techniques have meant that abortion is now seldom "necessary to

save the life of the mother"—if such necessity is construed in narrow terms.

At the same time medical progress has unearthed a new and important eugenic indication. Since 1941 it has been known and widely
accepted in the medical profession that at least 30 per cent of children whose mothers have German measles before the twelfth week
of pregnancy are born with congenital abnormalities—such as car-
diac lesions, microcephaly, congenital cataracts, or deafness. Many
physicians feel that a case of German measles warrants abortion,
even though the disease clearly presents no danger to the mother's
life. Hospitals do perform therapeutic abortions on such grounds;
this is one of the instances in which their practice directly violates
the statutory proscriptions. Prosecutors appear to be aware of such
practice, but apparently accept it, in effect concurring in the humanity of such a medical interpretation of the law.[11]

Another recent development has been an increased willingness to
grant therapeutic abortion on psychiatric grounds. This should not
be attributed solely to any supposed increase in mental disturbances
during pregnancy, nor even to mounting public awareness and acceptance of psychiatry. These may be relevant factors, but is is also
probable that the tendency of obstetricians to limit the granting of
abortion on medical grounds has led more and more women to look
to psychiatrists for help. A survey of therapeutic abortions performed
in 61 California hospitals during 1950 disclosed that the largest
number, approximately one fourth, was performed for reasons of
nervous and mental disease.[12] In New York City hospitals, the percentage of therapeutic abortions performed for psychiatric reasons
increased from 8 per cent in 1943 to 40 per cent in 1953.[13] The rise
in abortions for psychiatric reasons, however, has not been great
enough to offset the pronounced over-all decrease in the granting of
hospital abortions.

The evaluation of possible psychiatric indications for abortion
poses some extremely perplexing problems. A hospital that wishes
to abide by the letter of the law—in a *necessary-to-save-the-mother's-
life* state—may grant an abortion on psychiatric grounds only in
cases in which the woman presents a very convincing threat of suicide. Needless to say, there is no completely or even highly reliable
way of determining which of the women threatening suicide would

really execute their expressed intent. Furthermore, frequently—if not typically—a woman desperately seeking an abortion will claim life is no longer worth living, even if she has no strong self-destructive intentions or tendencies. On the other hand, because pregnancy is a period of both physiological and psychological reorientation, the possibility of serious depression is always present. Such a reaction may well be exacerbated when inadequate financial means or other pressing socioeconomic difficulties cause the woman to seek an abortion. Usually a mere state of depression will not be accepted as sufficient grounds for abortion. Yet, as some psychiatrists stress, the hospital's refusal to grant an abortion doesn't mean that the woman will then decide to have the child after all. Frequently the psychiatrist will encounter a woman whose psychopathological symptoms, as such, appear minor but whose determination to have an abortion is strong. Most hospitals will not take such determination into account in considering an application for abortion. To do so, it is felt, would amount to stretching the psychiatric indications to permit abortion on request. Yet it can be argued that the determination to abort at all costs, at least where evident to the psychiatrist at the time of consultation, might well be considered a relevant factor in the assessment of such cases. On the other hand, as one psychiatrist who has emphasized this point notes, there are some patients who are—through superficial supportive psychotherapy—readily enabled to carry the child to term. He mentions a case in which the woman came to him even though claiming to have already made arrangements for an illegal abortion. He suggests that she probably would not have done this if her wish to bear the child had not been stronger than her wish to abort—despite the fact that on impulse she might have actually gone through with the abortion.[14]

In recommending legal abortions, the psychiatrist faces the additional problem of hostility—or at least scepticism—on the part of the other medical men who may be involved in ruling on his cases. Thus obstetricians may feel that psychiatric diagnoses are being used as subterfuges in instances where abortion is not really justified, and they often are particularly unconvinced by assertions (which the psychiatrist may feel compelled to make) that the patient is likely to commit suicide if pregnancy is not terminated.[15]

The question of whether or not socioeconomic factors should receive consideration complicates the determination of psychiatric grounds for abortion. Some medical men feel that it is improper to allow such factors to influence the decision. It has even been suggested that doctors considering applications for abortion should do so without reference to any nonmedical data, so that a medical decision cannot be used to solve a social or economic problem. Others recognize that medical diagnoses, particularly psychiatric ones, must take account of the patient's total life situation. As one gynecologist puts it: "Admonishing physicians for permitting social and economic factors to influence their decisions indicates a blindness toward the modern concept of social medicine which embraces all aspects of sickness and health." [16] It may be worth noting that in Scandanavian countries there has been a willingness to grant legal abortion for "worn-out housewife's neurasthenia"—which is recognized as a fairly well-defined and serious psychosomatic disorder.[17] Such a diagnosis would not justify abortion under American laws, although similar conditions are taken into account by some practitioners in this country and the diagnosis of "reactive depression" may sometimes refer to essentially the same sort of condition.

Many individual practitioners also favor granting abortion on "humanitarian" grounds—as when pregnancy results from rape or incest, or among young unmarried girls—even though such abortions are illegal under current statutes.[18] In their recent survey of California hospitals, Packer and Gampell asked respondents to approve or disapprove therapeutic abortions in a number of hypothetical cases. One involved a fifteen-year-old minister's daughter who was raped (while on the way home from school) by an escapee from an institution for mental defectives. Psychiatrists had described her emotional distress and had recommended an abortion. As the authors note, there is no particular legal justification for abortion in such a case. Yet, fifteen hospitals approved a therapeutic abortion. Seven disapproved, three of these reporting that the case would stand a good chance of approval at another reputable hospital. Twenty-seven individual doctors approved, and only four disapproved. Of course it is true that this is a hypothetical case, that the situation is "loaded" by inclusion of numerous justifying factors, and that the responses may reflect personal inclination and not official hospital policy. Nonetheless, when asked specifically about the actual performance of illegal operations, eighteen of twenty-four hospitals replied that they believed they had authorized therapeutic abortions which did not strictly conform to their understanding of the law; only six reported that they had never done so.[19]

Under existing legal norms, then, hospital staff will often be driven into either of two undesirable situations: performance of an operation in deliberate violation of the law; or refusal to perform an operation which, according to their best medical judgment, is indicated. There are no systematic data regarding the extent to which hospital decisions on abortions reflect pressure from enforcement authorities or other public agencies. Some such pressure undoubtedly exists. It may be general and indirect—as when hospitals exercise constant caution lest their abortion rates elicit notice and critical comment by local or state officials. Or there may be more specific and direct pressure—as when a prosecutor warns a particular doctor to be more "careful" in granting abortions.[20] Guttmacher, a vociferous opponent of existing laws, has noted that even if the hospital administrator personally feels that his right to make medical decisions is improperly limited by an existing statute, he must attempt to adhere to the law. Caution in this regard may enable him, without jeopardizing the hospital's reputation, occasionally to depart from the letter of the law—as is frequently done, for example, in the German measles situation.[21]

ADMINISTRATIVE CONTROL

Many hospitals have now established some administrative machinery for dealing with requests for abortion, although there remains considerable variation in the specific procedures adopted. A survey of hospital requirements for permission to abort a patient during the year 1950 in California revealed the following procedures: consultation with one other physician (13 hospitals); consultation with two or more other physicians (41); review by special committee (11); and review by chief of staff or medical director (12). More recent statistics from California (published in 1959) showed that fifteen of twenty-six reporting hospitals (58 per cent) used some form of abortion committee, six having instituted such a device "in the last five years."[22] Illustrating the operation of abortion boards is the set of procedures introduced at New York City's Mount Sinai Hospital in 1952. There the chairman of the committee is the director of the obstetrical and gynecological service. The other members are the chief or a senior physician from the departments of pediatrics, medicine, surgery, and neuropsychiatry. In support of an application for abortion there must be two letters from consultants in the field involved. One of these consultants must also come before the committee, as must the obstetrician-gynecologist who will perform the abortion. If any member of the committee votes in the negative, the application is denied. As the former chairman of this board has pointed out, the board system—wherever introduced—has brought about a material reduction in the number of requests for therapeutic abortion because it becomes known that cases of questionable merit are unlikely to receive accreditation. He concludes: "No system to handle therapeutic abortion is ideal, but the board system has the advantage of consultation among several senior physicians and does not depend upon the views of one or two who frequently may have personal interests in affirmative decisions." [23]

From a sociological standpoint, this device for the self-regulation of legally questionable professional behavior is an interesting one. The procedure is efficient and objective, but it also is a technique for easing the uncertain position of the hospital administrator and emphasizes the need to preserve the reputation of the hospital and the obstetrical service.

Confronted with recurring demands for abortion, the medical practitioner is placed in a situation of "structured strain"—involving, among other things, "the tension between client interests and community interests." As Goffman notes, in this case "there is an out, an abortion often being defined as not in the 'best' interests of the person seeking it. . . ." [24] Many physicians, however, agree with the patient's assessment of her best interests rather than with the conflicting legal interpretation. For such physicians, the legal definition may not provide a satisfactory out, and recourse to administrative control is necessary to relieve the strain of decision. In the recent California study, hospital respondents were asked their views on the functions of abortion committee procedures. The function most frequently cited was that of policing the activities of the physician who might otherwise bring himself and his colleagues into disrepute. A large number of respondents also saw the committee as a device for insulating the individual obstetrician from the pressures of patients and colleagues, and for transferring to a collective body the onus of rejecting abortion applications. Some respondents agreed that the committee served to curb overly liberal obstetricians; only one viewed the committee mainly as a device for preventing the performance of illegal operations.[25] The board system may therefore prove highly functional for the physician who faces pressure from all sides on the abortion question. On the other hand, knowledge that the woman turned down by the board may well go on to obtain an illegal abortion prevents even this system from lifting the burden from the conscientious and ethical physician.[26]

So far, therapeutic abortion has been considered only as a hospital problem. Actually there is nothing in the law governing abortion that specifically precludes therapeutic abortion by an individual practitioner, provided the stipulated medical necessity is present. But even if he obtains prior approval from several consulting physicians, the individual doctor can never be certain that his decision would be upheld in court should any legal action be taken against him. It is true that in an abortion prosecution, the state must usually prove not only that the operation was performed but also that it was not necessary to preserve the mother's life. However, lenient rules regarding evidence in abortion cases considerably lessen the state's burden. Usually it is enough to show that the woman was healthy and in a normal condition prior to the operation to raise the inference that the operation was not necessary to preserve her life. In one federal case the court even required the physician to prove necessity as an affirmative defense:

> The performance of an abortion for any of these purposes [to avoid social disgrace, poverty, or illegitimacy] is so offensive to our moral conception that it does not seem unjust to put on the defendant who has committed an abortion the burden of producing evidence that the act was justified on therapeutic grounds.[27]

Abortion cases seldom come to the attention of law enforcement authorities except when death or hospitalization results. But since both dangers are always present, individual practitioners are often reluctant to take a chance and risk discovery, even when they are sympathetic to the woman's request. They are particularly reluctant to act when they can pass on the responsibility for decision to a hospital board, thus demonstrating to the patient a desire to help but running no personal risk. Of course the case of a woman whose application seems justified but has no chance of approval by a board, or who has already been turned down by such a board, continues to pose serious ethical dilemmas for doctors. In such situations, some frequently refer the woman to known abortionists; others will, on occasion, perform the operation themselves. The Kinsey data on illegal abortions revealed that many of the reported operations were performed by reputable physicians—as personal favors for relatives, friends, or other patients. "It is our conclusion that almost every general practitioner has been asked to perform an illegal abortion some time in his practice." [28]

INEQUITABLE TREATMENT

Not all unwillingly pregnant women have an equal opportunity to receive hospital-approved abortions. For one thing, socioeconomic status seems to make a difference. One report on therapeutic abortions in New York City hospitals noted that the ratio of such operations to live births in private hospitals is almost double that in voluntary (nonprofit) hospitals. Furthermore, a similar difference is found between the private and clinical services of voluntary institutions. The city hospitals have the lowest ratio—about one fifth that in the private hospitals and lower even than that for the general service in the voluntary hospitals. Similarly it was reported that at one particular institution, New York Hospital, there were no abortions for psychiatric indications on the ward service during 1941-44 and 0.1 abortion per 1000 live births during 1951-54. On the private service of the same hospital (for the same two periods), abortions performed for psychiatric indications went up from 1.8 to 4.1 per 1000.[29] According to competent reports, the private patient almost invariably receives greater consideration than the clinic patient, even though the former has the money to secure a relatively competent and safe illegal abortion should that need arise.[30]

Various observers have also noted that the unmarried woman

stands much less chance of obtaining a therapeutic abortion than the married one. This is not surprising, given the prevailing outlook on unmarried mothers. Not only does the social definition of their condition as "shameful" deter such women from seeking hospital help, but if they do seek such help the likelihood is they won't get it. Most hospital abortion boards will be extremely wary of granting abortions in any cases where the primary indication is nothing more than the humanitarian one of avoiding unwed motherhood.

Another practice viewed by some commentators as inequitable or harsh is the insistence, in many cases, that the woman obtaining a therapeutic abortion agree to undergo sterilization at the same time. Referring to some patients who had obtained illegal abortions and who had subsequently borne children, one psychiatrist stated:

> If they had been therapeutically instead of criminally aborted they would probably have been sterilized. I would like to point that out, because the package (therapeutic abortion-sterilization) deal is so frequent. I therefore consider them fortunate to have been illegally rather than therapeutically aborted, and thus spared sterilization.[31]

This "package deal" has been variously interpreted. In the case of a poverty-stricken woman who has already borne many children, it can be viewed as a humanitarian and sensible contraceptive measure. On the other hand, reluctance to perform the abortion, and resentment against both the woman and the psychiatrist for putting him in a position where he must do so, may induce unconscious punitive attitudes among some physicians. The compelled sterilization may sometimes be a form of retaliation in such instances.

Self-Induced Abortion

One of the great dangers of severely limiting the performance of hospital abortions is that many women will themselves attempt to terminate their pregnancies. To some, self-induced abortion may seem a less shameful and frightening way of solving their problem than visiting a criminal abortionist. In other cases, lack of funds or knowledge of just where to turn may lead the woman to attempt the abortion herself. Although the popular press frequently paints a lurid picture of the professional abortionist and his activities, many women are probably unaware of the greater dangers involved in self-induced abortion. Such techniques as severe exercise, hot baths, falls down stairs, and manipulation of the abdomen are rarely successful in accomplishing their purpose unless undertaken so vigorously that they also seriously endanger the life of the woman herself. Chemicals taken orally—purgatives, pelvic and intestinal irritants, drugs stimulating contraction of the uterus, and poisons—are equally hazardous if taken in dosages large enough to abort the fetus. Attempts at laceration with a sharp object, obviously perilous, demonstrate the extreme desperation of some women. An early account of postabortal hospital patients cited the use of crochet hooks, nail files, syringe tips, nutcrackers, and knives, introduced into the uterus. A more recent report mentions hatpins, umbrella ribs, and pieces of wire.[32]

FREQUENCY OF ATTEMPTS

It is obviously very difficult to estimate the number of attempts at self-induced abortion. There is reason to believe that successful self-induction represents only a very small proportion of completed abortions. The Kinsey study of over 650 induced abortions noted that only 8-10 per cent were self-induced. It also revealed that few women deliberately attempted to injure themselves (by falling downstairs or by having somone hit them in the abdomen) in order to produce an abortion. In all the reported illegal abortions (self-induced and other) drugs effected the termination in only about 9 per cent of the cases, although there were, in many instances, unsuccessful attempts at drug-induced abortion before resorting to an operation. The evaluation of self-induced abortion is complicated by the fact that, according to much medical evidence, the woman who with any real ease induces her own abortion often could have been likely to abort spontaneously anyway. The Kinsey researchers refer to a particularly confused category of cases among Negro women of the lowest socioeconomic group, a high percentage of whom reported successful abortions through the drinking of such substances as water in which rusty nails had been soaked, ginger tea, turpentine, and laundry blue. Generally, in determining whether an abortion was really self-induced rather than spontaneous, the researchers went along with the woman's interpretation of the event. In these particular cases, however, the rather fanciful reports were treated as inaccurate though sincere, and the abortions involved were classified as spontaneous.[33]

If relatively few attempts at self-induced abortion are successful, it does not follow that such attempts are not frequent. Many of the cases in which women enter hospitals because of complications from an attempted or completed abortion appear to have involved self-induction. This group includes not only those women whose intention it is to abort themselves, but also those who simply try to induce bleeding or other symptoms which would justify or require surgical completion of the abortion. One doctor, reporting on some New York cases, noted that three quarters or more of seventy abortions reported to the legal authorities were self-induced. Similarly a medical report dealing with the District of Columbia stated that in that area most abortion cases resulting in serious complications were self-induced, and that increased efforts to suppress abortion might raise the rate of self-induction and possibly the abortion death rate as well.[34] The most experienced abortionist encountered by the Kinsey researchers stated that about 80 per cent of his patients had attempted, in one way or another, to induce abortion themselves before coming to him.[35]

It is unfortunate that the Kinsey study dealt mainly with cases of completed abortion, and hence threw only indirect light on the question of attempted self-abortion. At the very least, however, one can confidently say that women frequently attempt self-abortion before resorting to an illegal operation. Data from the study suggest that such attempts may be especially likely among women of lower socioeconomic status. Given the dangers inherent in self-induced abortion, and its evident relation to the availability of other (legal and illegal) abortion opportunities, it is clear that prevailing abortion policy discriminates most severely against those unwillingly pregnant women whose situations are the most distressing.

The Abortionist

Society's unwillingness to provide social and legal sanction for abortion has led to the growth of a thriving illicit traffic in such operations, and to the emergence of the "professional" criminal abortionist. An early discussion nicely summarized the strength of the abortionist's position and the way a social need propelled the development of illegal abortion machinery:

> An endless circle was . . . set in motion. The ready willingness of women to visit an abortionist brought him immense profits. A fraction of these profits made it possible to cause an abortion with a greater degree of safety to the woman and a smaller chance of exposure of either the woman or the doctor. This led to a further appeal to women who wished to bring an abrupt termination to their pregnancies. And so the chain was complete.[36]

There is little doubt that the abortionists' practice is extremely widespread in the United States today, although estimates on criminal abortion (which would include self-induced abortions as well as those performed by "professionals") are uncertain. One writer in 1951 estimated a minimum of 330,000 criminal abortions each year, of which at least 300,000 involved an abortionist.[37] This figure was based on an assumed grand total of a million abortions, about two thirds spontaneous and one third induced. Yet, as the abortion conference estimate cited (see p. 12) suggests, the total of induced abortions alone may be as high as a million; in that case the number of criminal abortions would be much higher than 330,000. It has been reported that police consider criminal abortion the third biggest illegal endeavor in the United States, surpassed only by gambling and narcotics,[38] and experts claim that criminal abortionists exist in almost every city (perhaps even every town) throughout the country.

Conflicting statements have been made concerning the training, skill, and motives of the professional abortionist. Some accounts insist that most illegal abortions are performed by persons who have no medical training, and refer to such persons as "butchers" or "mechanics." There is little doubt that some professional abortionists do fall into this category. On the other hand, there are abortionists who are fully trained physicians. It is well-known that the physician who for one reason or another has lost his license to practice medicine, and the foreign-trained doctor who experiences difficulty in being admitted to practice in this country, may be especially likely to turn to an illegal abortion practice. There are also trained physicians who drift into illegal abortion work gradually, usually beginning with the performance of abortions as favors to their legitimate patients. Some physicians simply enter the field because of the lure of easy money.[39] It is sometimes suggested that there are special psychological reasons which propel a given physician into abortion practice, but the substantiation of such claims appears rather meager.

VARIATIONS IN SKILL

There is no way of accurately gauging the relative proportions of physician and nonphysician abortionists. In the Kinsey survey, women reporting illegal abortions indicated that about 85 per cent had been performed by physicians. Probably there were some instances in which women reported as physicians persons who were not actually licensed practitioners. Furthermore, Kinsey's general sample was biased toward those groups of women who would best be able to obtain competent abortion services. In addition, many of the illegal abortions reported in this study were performed without cost, or at least by doctors who had legitimate medical practices. As a result, the findings may exaggerate the actual participation by licensed physicians in regular abortion work. Nonetheless, the data from this study do suggest that some abortionists are well-trained, skilled medical men. On the basis of interviews with a limited number of professional abortion specialists, the Kinsey team reported being impressed with their technical ability and with the low number of reported deaths and other complications from their operations. They even cited the case of one specialist (with a fairly well-supported claim of having performed 30,000 abortions without a single death) who tried, unsuccessfully, to hire a psychiatric social worker to counsel prospective patients. More generally, these researchers emphasized that although the profit motive obviously may lead a doctor into an abortion practice, those they interviewed displayed a higher degree of medical qualification than earlier accounts had led them to expect.[40]

These conclusions, however, might not apply to a true sample of professional abortionists. As the Kinsey researchers pointed out, it would be highly useful to secure data from a large number of such practitioners, but the difficulties involved in doing so are fairly obvious.

Even if it is impossible to determine the extent of medical accreditation among abortionists, it is clear that at least the more skilled among them can claim an indirect link with legitimate medical practice—in that a considerable proportion of their patients have been referred to them by licensed physicians. This point was discussed at the Planned Parenthood Federation's 1955 conference on abortion by a once-licensed doctor who for some twenty years had carried on an illegal abortion practice in Baltimore. He asserted that there were 353 doctors in that community whom he had served for many years, and from many of whom he actually had signed letters of referral. He claimed further that when he had been brought to trial on abortion charges, he refrained from implicating any of these physicians. They, on the other hand, refused to support him in any way, and a few were actually instrumental in bringing about his conviction.[41] If this story is true, and there is little reason to doubt it, it nicely points up the ambivalent attitude of the medical profession on the abortion issue.

This case also suggests the highly ambiguous professional status of the skilled abortionist. The nonmedical abortionist, who clearly defines himself as an illicit practitioner and who is so defined by the public at large, may experience somewhat less role confusion than the one who is medically trained. The nonmedical abortionist is less concerned about being labeled a criminal, he has no formal medical credentials to lose, he makes no pretense to medical competence. He may associate with various disreputable individuals who serve to confirm and support his deviant self-image. The medical man who takes up an abortion practice, however, may often be torn between conflicting images of his professional and social self. He is more likely than his nonphysician counterparts to desire the esteem of, and contact with, legitimate practitioners. He still considers himself a doctor, and only with the greatest reluctance can he accept the fact that many consider him to be a criminal. He feels some real concern for the plight of his patients, and is anxious to exercise due care in their treatment—something he is not always able to do if he is at the same time to insure his own safety from detection and prosecution. Although he feels he performs a useful function both for his patients and for his legitimate professional colleagues, he knows that when the chips are down he will receive little open support.

DANGERS OF ILLEGAL ABORTION

It may be useful at this point to comment briefly on the question of the deaths that occur in illegal abortions. Early estimates placed the annual number of such deaths in this country at 8000 or more. As late as 1951, one expert suggested there still might be 5000-6000 such deaths annually.[42] The use of antibiotics and the exercise of increased care have clearly decreased the likelihood of death from criminal abortion. Statistics on known abortion deaths in New York City show a steady declining trend, from 144 deaths in 1921 to 15 in 1951. Commenting on these figures, the city's chief medical examiner stated: "I believe there are just as many abortions being done, but that they are being done under better conditions." He also noted some interesting breakdowns of these statistics: a disproportionate number of the women who died from abortions were Negroes, and although more of the women who underwent abortions were married, there were "more deaths from crudely done criminal abortion with very severe injury" among those who were single.[43] These data indicate the relatively more desperate plight of the single woman. She is more likely than the married woman to expose herself to a crude abortionist, and if postabortal complications develop, she is apt to wait longer before seeking medical help.

There are cases in which the inept technique of an unskilled abortionist directly leads to death. But even the fairly conscientious abortionist works under imperfect conditions, and must for his own safety get the woman to leave his place of work as soon after the operation as possible. Hence the inadequacy of aftercare, the frequent lack of necessary medicines and emergency equipment, and the dangers inherent in the abortion itself (at least when the abortionist has not had the proper training) combine to make criminal abortion highly dangerous even today. The immediate dangers and primary causes of death are shock, hemorrhage, embolism, infection, and poisoning.

Certain illegal abortion techniques may pose special dangers. For instance, injection of potassium soap compounds into the uterus by pressure syringe may be extremely dangerous. These pastes have been available "on the open market, . . . being sold ostensibly for use as antiseptics and not as abortifacients . . ." despite federal prosecutions under misbranding provisions of the federal Food, Drug and Cosmetic Act.[44]

Another popular abortion procedure has been the insertion into the uterus of a catheter—an elongated, tubular instrument often made of rubber or fiber. Left in the uterus, it acts as an irritant. This technique is sometimes used even in the late months of pregnancy. It has been widely used in New York City, often in such a way as to facilitate "getting around the law." The abortionist inserts a catheter and, knowing that bleeding may not start for some time, immediately sends the woman home with instructions to return when she begins to bleed. If by chance his office is raided during her return visit, the abortionist can claim that he was merely treating her for the bleeding. Usually the woman will uphold his story.[45]

FEES

In the Kinsey sample most illegal abortions were reported to have been operative (i.e., dilatation and curettage) and, as already noted, performed by physicians. These factors would minimize the risk of death or serious complications, but the limitations of the sample make it impossible to infer that most criminal abortions are now being performed under these relatively favorable conditions. As suggested earlier, the woman's socioeconomic status will help to determine the legal and illegal treatment she receives. One commentator has suggested that the distinction between "therapeutic" and "illegal" abortion represents merely a financial artifact: "in many circumstances the difference between the one and the other is $300 and knowing the 'right' person." [46] The opportunities for illegal treatment are also determined largely by finances. As Guttmacher has emphasized, the quality of illegal abortion services varies directly with the amount paid. While a five-dollar job (performed by an untrained operator) is quite likely to be bungled and to lead to serious complications or even death, the patient able to pay a large sum of money (say, a thousand dollars) can obtain the services of a skilled physician.[47]

Not only does this ability-to-pay criterion lead to less competent and safe treatment for working-class women, but it also introduces the irony that the well-to-do woman with "connections" may be more likely to encounter the sympathetic practitioner who will charge only a reasonable (for her) fee. It is noteworthy that the Kinsey sample, which overrepresented the higher socioeconomic categories, contained quite a few cases of abortions performed free of charge— presumably as a favor by a family physician. The fees paid by these women do not appear excessive. Excluding all abortions secured without cost, the median amounts paid for illegal operative abortions were: $84 for single women, $77 for the married ones, and $98 for the previously married.[48] The working-class or lower-middle-class woman, on the other hand, will often obtain the services of an unscrupulous operator who is really out to get all he can. Thus although the fees may increase in absolute terms with increases in the clients' socioeconomic position (some of the Kinsey data indicate that this is the case), the relative deprivation may actually be greater in the lower strata.

The woman seeking an abortion is usually in no position to argue strongly about the fee:

Criminal abortionists charge as much as $2000—whatever the traffic will bear. Today the average fee in Chicago is $400 or $500. It is more in New York. In Los Angeles a midwife charges $25; a male nurse, $100; a chiropractor, $150 to $200; and a medical doctor or osteopath, at least $500. The highest price known there in recent years is $1800, and $1000 is not uncommon. . . .[49]

One report asserted that in 1941 an abortion specialist with a normal business could be expected to earn about $25,000 a year, while doctors with higher-income clientele were earning from $150,000 to $200,000.[50]

Illegal Organization

It is not at all surprising that an illegal business with such potentially high profits should, at least in part, be well organized. The modifying phrase *at least in part* is necessary to indicate that illicit abortion services are not controlled by a monolithic criminal organization and to take into account that different types of individuals perform these services under a wide variety of circumstances. Except for the legitimate practitioner who occasionally performs an abortion for a patient or friend, it should be evident that the nature of abortion practice invariably implies a certain amount of organization. To be successful, the abortionist requires adequate equipment, a place in which to work, and some technical or other assistance. Potential customers must learn of his existence and location, yet at the same time a certain amount of anonymity must be maintained. Some means of avoiding police interference must also be developed —whether it be the elaboration of an extremely convincing front, a continuous shifting of location, or a direct or indirect financial arrangement with the authorities.

Given these imperatives, highly elaborate behavior systems have developed in the abortion profession. One report noted the existence in New York City of two "fairly complex social structures," the abortion "mill" and the abortion "ring." The mill involved one or more abortionists permanently located and aborting about a dozen women daily. The ring consisted of "a number of interacting abortionists or mills working intermittently at several occasionally changing locations and aborting an even more considerable number of women daily. . . . Clients are accommodated at the various locations depending on the pressure of referrals, the availability of operators at the moment of need, and the ability of the client to pay. . . ."[51]

Although *mill* may not seem a properly nonmoralistic designation, this term, apparently adopted from enforcement parlance, does point up the organized nature and continually high rate of activity of even the smaller of the two types of enterprises. According to Bates, the physician whose abortion practice is large and well-organized enough to fall into the mill category is likely to employ a business staff as well as medical assistants. Besides a secretary-receptionist, there may often be a business agent or manager. The business agent handles dealings with the landlord, and the payment of salaries, bills, bribes, and split fees. He may also function as contact man between the abortionist and the various sources of referral. Some large mills have also been known to employ "runners" to bring sources of referral into contact with the business agent. Bates notes that because of the confidential nature of the job, the abortionist may employ as business manager a relative or closely trusted friend. In the cases he studied, the business agent invariably had either a degree in law or at least some legal training (probably to provide for future contingencies).[52]

Bates lists the local druggist, the general practitioner, and previous patients as the primary sources of referral to a mill, and includes taxidrivers and bellboys as secondary sources. The role of the legitimate physician in effecting referrals should not be underestimated; recall the case of the physician-abortionist who had "served" over 350 practitioners in his city (*see* p. 27). Individual patterns of referral are determined largely by the prospective client's economic and social situation. The woman of means obtains better illegal services partly because she gains the assistance of a reputable doctor who can often refer her to a competent physician-abortionist. The woman of lower socioeconomic status will usually have to rely on general word-of-mouth referrals in her neighborhood or on the secondary sources mentioned above, and is correspondingly more likely to be referred to a less competent abortionist.

Frequently some sort of respectable front is used to shield the illicit practice. The abortionist may adopt some seemingly proper designation to cover, yet also hint at, the real character of his activities. According to Rongy *office gynecology* was once the "casually accepted medical term for the abortionist," recognized by every practitioner.[53] Similarly, in a California case, a card on the door of the defendant's apartment indicated that he was engaged in "phys-iotherapy and spot reducing." [54] At times the front becomes ex-panded, as in the case of an enterprise conducted by two women, one of whom was a Peruvian doctor, though neither had a license to practice medicine in New York:

> The Peruvian led a double life. She posed as a respectable director of the Inter-American Cultural School which she operated at her pa-latial private residence on Fifth Avenue. This fancy front was main-tained with revenues derived from the performance of abortions at her co-defendant's home. The abortion clientele consisted almost en-tirely of poor, Spanish-speaking people, who looked up to the affluent Peruvian because she lived on Fifth Avenue and associated with lead-ers in the Latin-American community.
>
> The conspirators had a complicated code system for telephone con-versations. Patients were *packages. Six pairs of nylons* or *eight pairs of nylons* meant that the patient was six to eight weeks pregnant. Information concerning a patient's financial status was imparted by terms such as *special delivery,* which indicated ability to pay double the usual fee, or *parcel post,* meaning a moderate increase over the usual charge.[55]

A code of this sort is but one of many precautionary measures utilized by abortionists. Equipment may be kept under cover—a portable folding operating table, a sterilizer ingeniously hidden somewhere in the office. This office may, as already mentioned, be shifted from place to place, and often the abortionist comes to his place of work only for scheduled operations. Anonymity is a per-vasive concern, in the interest of which the patient may be blind-folded, various devices such as surgical masks or operating table screens may be used to shield the abortionist's identity, and direct conversations between the two will be avoided. Under the system recently described by a New York observer, a woman wanting an abortion calls one doctor, who arranges for another doctor (whom she does not know)—perhaps accompanied by a nurse—to come to her home by appointment and to perform the abortion there.[56] This technique seems roughly analogous to the *modus operandi* of call girls. Although it may represent a relatively costly procedure for obtaining illicit services, a mobile and anonymous pattern of this sort certainly minimizes the risk of legal interference. Whatever the specific procedures adopted by a criminal abortionist, his behavior will always exhibit elements of what Bates calls "defensive social adaptation." As he notes: "Since attack from any legitimate or predatory source threatens the social and economic adjustment of mill functionaries, one is not surprised to find them taking energetic countermeasures both on a planned and emergent basis." [57]

POLICE CORRUPTION

One type of countermeasure involves the payment of "protection" money to law enforcement officers. It seems reasonable to assume such payment on the part of abortionists who operate "undetected" for any length of time in a metropolitan location. On the other hand, the abortionist who is constantly on the move and who utilizes numerous intermediaries and elaborate codes probably has not purchased police protection—if he had, such measures would not be necessary. One commentator has stated that, on the whole, abortion is probably less protected than either gambling or prostitution.[58] There is no way of knowing what proportion of abortionists fall into these different categories. It may be that there has been an increase in the mobile system, which abortionists might find safer than reliance on regular police protection. However, according to another account, supposedly based on an abortionist's own experiences:

> One reason fees are high is because the patient must absorb the payoff to police and top officials. Abortionists tell of judges, lawyers, jailers, and police whom they pay for protection, some of whom have brought their wives, daughters, or mistresses to the abortionist. Graft is accepted by all abortionists as a necessary annoyance and added expense passed on to the patient.[59]

Many law enforcement personnel share the widespread belief that the abortionist is in fact performing a useful service, and are also well aware of the public indifference to strong enforcement of this particular law. Under such conditions it is relatively easy, as an early analysis pointed out, "for officials to convince themselves that there is nothing morally reprehensible in accepting bribes or protection money from abortionists." [60] Some law enforcement officials insist there is no longer widespread police corruption connected with abortion. But there is little doubt that the abortionist continues to present an inviting prospect for extortion by the police as well as by others.

Quite elaborate procedures may be used to exert pressure on the illegal abortionist—one of which involves a female decoy and a carefully rehearsed "raid" of the premises by actual or impersonated detectives. The abortionist has no way of knowing whether the raid is legitimate or not, and often he will jump at the opportunity to buy his way out. Payments made on such occasions have been known to run as high as a thousand dollars per "raider." [61]

Law Enforcement

It is widely recognized that the laws against abortion are highly unenforceable. Over the years, the annual number of prosecutions and convictions has been negligible. Along with his estimate of over 300,000 criminal abortions performed annually, Fisher held that the annual number of convictions might be less than 1000. He concluded: "It is doubtful if any other felonious act is as free from punishment as criminal abortion." [62] Occasionally law enforcement authorities in a particular area will make a special effort to apprehend criminal abortionists. For example, during the years of 1946-53 the office of the District Attorney in New York County prosecuted 136 cases of abortion, a very high proportion of which resulted in conviction on one or more of the offenses charged in the indictment. However, as has been pointed out elsewhere, this figure must represent but a tiny fraction of the abortions occurring in the country during that period. Furthermore, in a high percentage of the cases, the defendants received suspended sentences.[63]

Even such a concerted effort, then, can only be expected to scratch the surface of the illegal abortion problem. Most law enforcement officials recognize the determination of unwillingly pregnant women to obtain abortions, law or no law. As a result, law enforcement goals are—in practice—limited to the control of abortion rather than to its elimination. As has been shown, self-induced abortion is probably widespread. Yet the prosecutor ordinarily does not consider it a phenomenon with which he must be concerned. Likewise, although some states make it a crime for a woman to submit to an abortion, women have traditionally been immune from prosecution in abortion cases. There is no record of reported American cases involving conviction of a woman for submitting to an abortion. Hospitals, which contravene the abortion laws from time to time, also are—within broad limits—free from prosecution. Similarly, the legitimate medical practitioner may perform an occasional abortion without anticipating legal difficulties—provided the operation does not result in the woman's death or hospitalization. A large number of professional abortionists may also manage to avoid detection. The fact is that the extent of abortion practice is so great, and available police manpower is so far below the level needed even to try to curb it, that the urban prosecutor confines his efforts to building up a case against a few of the more notorious offenders.

OBTAINING EVIDENCE

To uncover and prosecute successfully the organized abortionist is a formidable task. Women who visit abortionists do not want to talk about the experience. Even when they feel no compelling desire to protect the abortionist, they fear adverse publicity for themselves. In some states they may also fear self-incrimination, notwithstanding the fact that they would rarely encounter serious legal difficulties. Newspapers in some cities have aided prosecutors by adopting the policy of omitting the names of the patients from their stories on abortion cases. Furthermore, in some jurisdictions a woman who is known to have submitted to an abortion may be compelled to testify provided she is granted immunity from subsequent prosecution.[64] But few women come voluntarily to the police to tell about their abortions, and usually an illicit operation comes to light only when hospitalization results. Ordinarily a hospital will report the admission for treatment of a patient who seems to have undergone an abortion. In New York City a special regulation requires hospitals to report "any case of abortion or miscarriage where criminal practice is discovered or suspected." [65] Aside from the ethical considerations involved in making such reports of medical information, this practice is subject to the fallibility and variation of individual reaction. In the absence of definite signs of instrumentation, doctors may very likely disagree as to whether or not a particular woman has undergone an abortion. This uncertainty is heightened by the unwillingness of most women to admit, even to doctors, that they submitted to an illegal operation. For example, postabortion patients in New York appear to know about the special reporting requirement and are reluctant to answer the doctor's inquiries fully and truthfully. As a result, it is unlikely that much reliable information has been obtained through this procedure.[66]

Most abortion information comes to the prosecutor through the death of the woman or through clear evidence of criminal abortion in a woman who has subsequently been hospitalized. Once such a lead is obtained, female investigators may be sent to the suspect's office to see whether he will agree to perform an abortion. However, willingness to perform the operation is usually insufficient for criminal liability. In a California case, for example, the court dismissed convictions on three counts of attempted abortion because defendants had gone no further than "mere preparation." [67]

The most fruitful device for obtaining the necessary evidence is a well-timed, well-organized raid, as illustrated by the comprehensive technique developed by District Attorney Frank Hogan in New York.[68] Once a lead is obtained, detectives keep the suspect's office under constant surveillance. In one case where a series of raids eventually smashed a $500,000 a year abortion mill, investigators masqueraded as taxi drivers and maintenance men in order to watch the apartment house in question. After a careful watch has indicated that the suspect is performing abortions, detectives, an assistant district attorney, the district attorney's medical advisor, and other staff members may join in an unexpected "visit" to the suspect's place of business. If their timing is off, the raid may uncover nothing suspicious. But if an operation is in progress the chances of getting evidence are good. The medical advisor is on hand to give the woman any treatment she may need and to locate any instruments or other telltale signs of abortion. A female member of the staff may also go along—primarily to be with the patient, who is likely to become somewhat upset by the raid. Several detectives are assigned to look for records and files—a particularly important procedure, for records may disclose the names of other patients who could be called to testify, the dates of operations already performed, the fees collected or due (probably not often the latter, for abortionists usually demand advance payment), and any sources of referral. Efforts may be made to get a blood sample from the woman and a urine specimen for a pregnancy test. If the operation has already been performed, the blood sample may be particularly helpful for comparison with blood stains found near the operating area.

Through such a procedure the prosecution may come into court with a fairly strong case. Yet abundant evidence does not necessarily insure a conviction. As noted earlier, the state usually will have to prove not only that the operation was performed but also that it was not medically necessary. This will be particularly difficult when the defendant is a licensed physician. Although most abortion laws do not specifically distinguish between operations by physicians and by laymen, in practice the courts do tend to make such a distinction: a presumption of good faith may be extended to a physician defendant. Juries are loathe to convict doctors and judges do not like to impose harsh sentences on them. Hence, as seen in the New York data cited above, many of those convicted may receive suspended sentences. A similarly empty gesture is the revocation of a physician-abortionist's medical license: an abortionist's reputation depends on his operating skill, not on his formal credentials. Nor is he likely to be cowed by the new possibility of prosecution for practicing medicine without a license, for he has already faced the far more serious charge connected with his illegal abortion practice.

UNENFORCEABLE LAWS

Unsatisfactory experience with the laws against abortion points up some of the major consequences of attempting to legislate against the crimes without victims. As an English legal authority states, unsuccessful laws against abortion illustrate "the inherent unenforceability of a statute that attempts to prohibit a private practice where all parties concerned desire to avoid the restriction." [69] It is evident that large numbers of persons, otherwise quite respectable, find themselves compelled—for a variety of reasons—to violate the proscription against abortion. Abortion is a private consensual transaction, a willing payment of money for (illicit) services rendered. Although some persons may view the aborted woman as the "victim" of the abortionist, the woman herself does not share this definition of the situation. Even where she has found the experience extremely distasteful or frightening—perhaps especially in such cases—she is most unlikely to wish to bring a complaint against the person who has performed the operation.

From a law enforcement standpoint, this lack of a complainant is crucial. The only possible law enforcement approach, particularly in view of the widespread reluctance to convict abortionists, is to concentrate on a small number of the more flagrant violators of the law, and to build up an airtight case in each instance. This involves, as shown earlier, long-term surveillance of selected suspects—a questionable use of valuable law enforcement manpower. It may also involve compelling the testimony of former clients who had thought that an extremely unpleasant life experience was over and done with. In cases of overzealous investigation, there may be searches and seizures of evidence that border on infringement of the suspect's constitutional guarantees.

As noted also, such a situation holds a clear-cut invitation to police corruption and to illegal exploitation by others as well. Because there are no data indicating a decline in the over-all abortion rate, and because there is a known tendency to grant fewer and fewer legal abortions, the only possible conclusion is that the demand is being deflected into illicit channels. Under current hospital policy, even the sophisticated woman of means and influence, who might once have been able to secure a "therapeutic" abortion, is now driven to the illegal abortionist. Because she can afford to pay an especially high price for his services, the entire illegal process may be enriched and strengthened. It is difficult not to conclude that the thriving illicit market is largely a direct result of the current restrictions on legal abortion. The efforts to combat abortion and the protective measures adopted by the abortionist provide a clear example of what Sutherland termed "the competitive development of techniques of crime and of protection against crime." [70] Repressive laws have nurtured the development of a well-organized criminal profession, which provides strongly demanded services at a high profit, using part of the profit to improve the services and to insulate itself from the negative reaction of official agencies.

Aftereffects of Abortion

Under proper hospital conditions and in the first few months of pregnancy, abortion is today a relatively simple procedure which should have no adverse medical consequences. Although there have been no empirical studies of public and professional attitudes in this area, widespread uncertainty about the safety of abortion techniques may well persist. In part, this uncertainty has been promoted by conflicting medical statements concerning the results of the program of free, legalized abortion instituted in the Soviet Union[71] shortly after the Bolshevik Revolution. The Soviet aim was to free women from the need to bear unwanted children, thus to enhance women's rights, and at the same time hopefully to reduce the number of illegal abortions and the high rates of mortality and morbidity associated with such operations. Some of the early reports concerning the program were highly favorable. On the other hand, by the 1930's even some of the Soviet medical statements indicated a high rate of undesirable side-effects attributable to the operations. There is still considerable doubt as to the actual extent of these complications, but at least one leading American commentator asserted that—despite a great decrease in abortion deaths—there was "a marked deterioration of the physical condition of the aborted woman." [72]

In 1936 the Soviet government sharply reversed its abortion policy, and the termination of pregnancies once again became illegal—except in cases of clear-cut medical necessity. The reasons for this shift in policy are not entirely clear. Many interpreters tended to attribute the change to the alleged bad aftereffects of abortion. Yet it is noteworthy that most such allegations were retrospective—statements such as that quoted above were made after the announcement of the shift in Soviet policy. It is also significant that this particular policy change was but one element in a broader pattern of reversal of policies relating to various aspects of family law—a pattern which also included, for example, tightening the regulations governing marriage and divorce. This fact lends support to the alternative thesis that the reversal of abortion policy was primarily a reflection of over-all changes in Soviet social policy rather than of specific medical consequences; a desire for increased population may well have been a major factor underlying this particular change.

In 1955 Russia once again legalized abortion. Asserting that henceforth the state would rely on education and propaganda to encourage motherhood and prevent unnecessary abortions, the government's 1955 edict also stated that "unceasing awareness and the rising cultural level of women" in every way of life made the policy change possible. A news account of the new law noted that, "by the end of 1955, the Government's drive to step up the birth rate through bachelors' taxes, family allotments, and other devices appears to have met with signal success. Indeed, the population increase is far outstripping the Government's ability to provide more housing, schools, and other facilities." [73]

The main issue raised in discussions of the Soviet experience has been the physical or physiological effects of abortion. It should be stressed that even if there was, in fact, a high rate of complications under the early Soviet program, many of the operations were performed without anesthesia under conditions which modern American practitioners would hardly approve. Hence such adverse reports are of questionable current relevance, and most experts assert that strictly medical complications from abortion now are rare. There is still, however, a strong current of professional opinion emphasizing the likelihood of adverse psychological consequences. One psychiatrist has gone so far as to insist that abortion "runs counter to the biological stream of life" and that therefore any abortion (except perhaps those performed to terminate pregnancies resulting from rape or incest) is likely to produce serious and adverse psychic aftereffects.[74]

PSYCHOLOGICAL CONSEQUENCES

This may be a somewhat extreme position, but psychiatrists of various orientations agree that abortion can, in many instances, have serious adverse psychological consequences. In her influential study, *The Psychology of Women,* Helene Deutsch notes that abortion may often produce immediate or delayed guilt feelings. For example, she cites one case of a woman who, on giving birth to a defective child two years after an abortion, became convinced that her "criminal deed" was responsible for this event. In another instance a woman who had undergone two abortions because of a physical condition later felt the need to erect tombstones for the fetuses. Deutsch concludes, on the basis of a large number of cases, that "at bottom there is hardly a woman who reacts to it [abortion] with complete realism even when the rationalization is the best possible one." It is significant, though, that the same author nonetheless refuses to view all decisions to abort as psychologically unsound. The decision of whether or not to preserve the child must often involve primarily an assessment of short-run favorable and unfavorable consequences; "the later dangers may be equally unavoidable whether the decision is positive or negative, and it is impossible to estimate in advance which danger will prove greater in each individual case." [75] Most psychiatrists seem to agree that every abortion is a psychologically disturbing event. Beyond that, their views cover a considerable range—from the belief that often the trauma of abortion will be less severe than that of bearing an unwanted child to the view that every decision to abort (with the possible exception of those involving cases of pregnancy through rape) constitutes a symptom of psychopathology.

It should be kept in mind that psychiatric reports of the adverse effects of abortion tend to be based on a rather selective sampling of aborted women. The psychiatrist usually learns only of the cases involving psychic complications. Research into the reactions of a broader range of aborted women is necessary in order to develop an accurate picture of the various types of consequences. To some extent this defect has been rectified by studies of women legally aborted in the Scandanavian countries. One such study—a follow-up on 479 women who had undergone therapeutic abortion on psychiatric grounds in Sweden—showed that two to three years after the operations, 75 per cent experienced no self-reproach, 14 per cent felt mild self-reproach, 11 per cent serious self-reproach, and 1 per cent had suffered an impairment of working capacity (but these were cases in which there were other contributing factors).[76] In another survey of 84 women aborted in the Stockholm area (it is not clear whether there was any respondent overlap in the two studies), 39 declared they were perfectly happy and satisfied at having had the abortion, and 45 were not completely happy about it—4 were embarrassed and distressed and did not like to talk about it, 9 were classified as consciously repressing feelings of guilt, and 10 were reported to have really suffered an impairment of mental health. A similar Norwegian study covering a carefully selected group of 88 legally aborted women disclosed only two cases in which the women showed any negative psychological reaction to the operation.[77]

These data suggest that when abortions are performed legally and in hospitals—at least in countries where a nonpunitive attitude toward abortion is widespread and even official—no serious adverse psychic consequences need be anticipated. Data collected by the Kinsey research group provide information about the reactions of a group of 442 white, nonprison women who had undergone illegal operations within an over-all context of strongly professed social condemnation.[78] About three fourths of the women reported that there were no unfavorable consequences—physical, psychological, social, or legal—resulting from the operation. A total of about 16 per cent reported some unfavorable physical consequence—only 7 per cent of which were classified as severe. A special comparative analysis of women aged twenty-six to thirty who had and who had not had previous abortions revealed, for this age group at least, no significant relation between induced abortion and subsequent sterility. Adverse psychological reactions were reported by less than 10 per cent of the women. Such reactions were usually described in general terms, as "emotional upset," "depression" or "guilt feelings"; a few women said they were "nervous" for some time after the abortion. In addition, "One regretted a subsequent sterility, one almost committed suicide, one reported that it affected her subsequent sexual relations adversely, another that she was 'ruined mentally.'" The authors summarize these findings by stating that there appeared to be little psychological trauma in the great majority of the cases, but a considerable amount of unfavorable reaction in a few cases. It was also found that a premarital induced abortion had not usually deterred a woman from continuing with premarital coitus, and that a premarital abortion did not adversely affect sexual adjustment in marriage as measured by the rate of orgasm in the first year of marital intercourse. Nor was there any evident relation between premarital abortion and the failure of subsequent marriages. Adverse social consequences of abortion were also minimal—such difficulties as gossip, rejection by family or friends, and having to leave school were reported in only about 3 per cent of the cases and only by single women. There was not a single case reported in the entire study of a woman encountering legal sanctions as a result of an illegal abortion.

It seems clear that the harmful consequences of abortion have often been exaggerated. Not only is there evidence to indicate that legal hospital abortions need produce few adverse aftereffects, but it also appears that many illegal abortions can be experienced without undue trauma. However, the Kinsey findings do not tell the whole story. As noted earlier, the sample in this study significantly over-represented those women in a position to secure relatively safe abortions at the hands of the less predatory illegal operatives. Furthermore, the reliability of the reports may have been impaired by such factors as the problems of recall and the failure to report difficulties which could have stemmed indirectly from the abortion but which were not obviously related to it. Nonetheless, the infrequency of serious disturbance directly caused by the abortion is impressive. (Limited to interview data, this study could not, of course, produce any direct evidence regarding death from abortion.) It is noteworthy, too, that "the great percentage of the women who had illegal abortion stated that it had been the best solution to their immediate problem." [79] This statement seems to express nicely the dominant reaction of unwillingly pregnant women who have aborted. Relatively few such women regret their abortions, in the sense of consciously wishing they had not obtained them. On the other hand, the operation invariably is viewed as a lesser evil rather than a positive good, and may almost always be a basis for considerable negative feelings expressed or felt in one way or another. The degree of negative feeling varies from individual to individual, and depends partly on the woman's general social position and the particular type of situation which impelled her to resort to abortion.

Abortion as a Social Situation

The picture of the abortion problem will be incomplete unless a further attempt is made to understand the behavior of those individuals involved. Unfortunately, there has been almost no systematic research into just how women think, feel, and act while they are engaged in the process of obtaining an abortion. Nor is there any detailed information about the sequences of steps taken by various categories of women in this process. Existing knowledge does, however, provide a considerable basis for constructing at least tentative formulations about these matters.

SOCIOECONOMIC STATUS

To begin with, it should be clear that the woman's socioeconomic status is significant in determining both her general reaction to the unplanned pregnancy and the specific steps she takes in dealing with it. In upper-class, "sophisticated" circles, an unwanted pregnancy may be viewed merely as an inconvenience. There may be some women in this category who can "handle" such a problem with relative ease and dispatch. As already noted, such women are in the best position to secure competent and perhaps even legal termination of pregnancy. The woman of less means and worldliness is much worse off. Although some women in the lowest socioeconomic levels may be so inured to misery that they accept unplanned pregnancy with resignation, it seems likely that there are many cases in which the woman is both deeply distressed by her pregnancy and well aware of her inability to "handle" the situation by herself. Such a woman finds herself in a position of great vulnerability. Not only is she dependent on others for help, but she faces the likelihood that those to whom she turns will prove inadequate to the task. As has already been shown, she may be especially likely to attempt self-abortion, often relying on old wives' tales about abortion methods. She may finally, and often at a dangerously late stage, make her way to an incompetent and unscrupulous abortionist operating in sordid surroundings. With either procedure, she faces a relatively strong chance of ending up with complications and possibly even in a hospital. In the latter case, she may be treated with less consideration than her upper-class counterpart. The nature of such an abortion-seeking process is, then, quite different from the somewhat less frantic, sordid, and dangerous (if no less determined) sequence of steps followed by the well-to-do woman. It would seem to follow from this difference in social procedures that women of differing socioeconomic positions would tend to define the process of seeking and obtaining an abortion differently. Given her usual high level of advantage and independence, the upper-class woman may regard the need to get an abortion, in some sense, as relatively more disruptive than the lower-class woman would. Yet the objective conditions facing the less affluent woman are certainly much harsher. In the absence of evidence to the contrary, it seems justifiable to think that—all other things being equal—negative feelings about the abortion situation will increase as one goes down the socioeconomic ladder.

MARITAL STATUS

Similarly, the woman's marital status will influence her reactions. By the very fact of her pregnancy, the single woman becomes a social deviant. As such she may enter the abortion-seeking process with special bitterness and desperation. This is particularly so because society has sanctioned, even encouraged, behavior of which premarital pregnancy is a foreseeable result. Of course the fact of premarital pregnancy must be considered together with socioeconomic status—the interaction or intersection of these factors produces a complicated set of differing responses to the situation. For example, a study of pregnancy outcomes among 572 nonprison

Negro women by the Kinsey team revealed that the single women with less than college education were far more likely to have live births and less likely to resort to induced abortion than were white respondents (in the main Kinsey sample) of the same educational level.[80] Similarly, in a special sample of 900 white female prison inmates, whom the Kinsey team regarded as representative of the lowest socioeconomic level (for which their sample was otherwise inadequate), they found a high premarital live birth rate and a low rate of induced abortion. This they attributed to a less strong disapproval of illegitimacy, as well as to the high cost of abortion, and a general distrust of physicians.[81]

Although this study did find a clear-cut inverse relation between educational level and premarital conception, the extent of the problem of premarital pregnancies should not be underestimated. Thus, among the total sample, it was found that by the age of forty, roughly 10 per cent had had a premarital pregnancy, regardless of their ultimate married status. As the authors noted, it is "clear that premarital pregnancy is an enormous social phenomenon that has involved not merely a few unfortunates, but millions of women. . . ." [82] For most unwillingly pregnant single women, abortion is the preferred "solution." In the Kinsey study, of 355 pregnancies that ended while the women were unmarried, 316 (89 per cent) terminated in induced abortion. Among the total sample of women aged thirty-six and over ("who may be said to have completed their premarital reproductive lives"), 8 per cent had experienced a premarital induced abortion. Of the women aged thirty-six or more who had premarital coitus prior to age thirty-six, some 18 per cent had had an induced abortion.[83]

The unmarried woman tends to be at a disadvantage both in her attempts to secure legal abortion and in her dealings with illegal abortionists. Because of this, and given her general desperation, the unmarried woman may find the abortion-seeking process a good deal more unpleasant than the married woman would—the latter, at any rate, always has the "respectable" alternative of bearing the unwanted child. The previously married woman who is unwillingly pregnant also is in a very awkward situation. As the Kinsey study noted, society makes no special provision for the pregnant divorcée or widow. Compared with the single woman, she has less opportunity and perhaps less desire for a "solution" through marriage, and she encounters strong social pressures driving her to the abortionist.[84]

INTERPERSONAL RELATIONS

All abortion-seekers face certain highly unpleasant experiences, whatever their social or marital status. One area of common experience concerns problems arising in connection with pre-existing close interpersonal relationships. When the father of the unwanted child is known and has been anything more than an incidental sex partner, the undesired pregnancy challenges the harmony of whatever relationship has existed. This is obviously so when the man disavows responsibility. In other cases the man may insist that the woman bear the child even though she does not really want it (this situation is probably rare). More often, the man convinces the woman to have an abortion, when her own feelings about the operation are at least mixed. In such cases, even though the woman may have felt from the start that an abortion is what she really wanted, some alteration in the relationship may occur.

> Even if both have weighed all the pros and cons and taken the decision together, their communion is broken afterward. Suddenly, the previous simple reasoning proves wrong; the woman realizes now that her agreement with her husband or lover regarding the abortion had an ambivalent quality.[85]

The woman may develop a strong resentment against the man in question or against men in general. A man, after all, was at least equally responsible for the predicament in which she found herself, yet she was the one who paid. Simone de Beauvoir has persuasively emphasized that the woman in this situation often sees herself as harshly victimized, soiled, and humiliated.[86]

This is not to say that bearing the child is necessarily a preferable choice either for the woman or from the standpoint of the relationship. And certainly the undesirability of bringing an unwanted child into the world is an important factor which must be taken into consideration in reaching a decision in such a situation. But it does seem evident that the decision to abort—even the need to consider abortion—will almost always place some serious strain on the relationship. Other interpersonal relationships may also pose problems for the woman contemplating or deciding upon abortion. Thus, the attitudes and behavior of close relatives and friends can have a crucial impact. A case has been cited of a woman whose father told her, following an induced abortion, that she had done a terrible thing and that as a result she probably would never be able to have a baby. Her subsequent guilt led to a succession of serious psychosomatic disorders and to two miscarriages.[87] Although this case seems extreme, it points up the significance that the reactions and comments of others may have.

DEALING WITH THE ABORTIONIST

Another common problem area for most women who seek an abortion involves the actual locating of, and dealing with, an illegal abortionist. The woman who is blindfolded and taken to a strange place where she must submit to a frightening ordeal at the hand of a masked stranger is bound to find the experience threatening and degrading. One psychiatrist notes that some such women determine that they will never again go through such an ordeal, "even if this means renouncing sexual activity." [88]

The Kinsey data suggest that such a strong reaction need not occur, but again it must be recognized that respondents in that survey probably had access to better-than-average abortion facilities. In any case, the absence of pronounced psychic disturbance does not mean that the experience itself was not a harrowing and demoralizing one. Just as there are many different kinds of persons performing illegal abortions under widely varying conditions, there is bound to be considerable variation in the kinds and degrees of shadiness and sordidness to which aborting women are subjected. However, apart from those women who obtain the abortion as a favor from an otherwise legitimate practitioner, at the very least a high degree of unpleasantness can be expected in all illegal abortion situations. Much of this unpleasantness stems from the inescapable fact of the woman's extreme dependence and vulnerability. The woman is pre-pared to do almost anything to achieve her purpose, and as a result she is open to various types of exploitation.

Undoubtedly the dominant type of exploitation is financial. A large proportion of illegal abortions appear to be preceded by con-siderable haggling and bargaining over fees, and the unscrupulous abortionist will "take" the woman for all he can get. Apart from any actual financial hardship this process may cause, it can hardly help but be demoralizing to the woman that her pregnancy and her difficult decision to terminate it are now treated as the basis for a not-even-courteous business transaction.

Sexual exploitation is another real possibility. Although there are —understandably—no systematic data on this point, cases involving improper advances and actual sexual demands have been mentioned by some observers.

Threats, cruelty, and various sorts of manhandling, as well as a good deal of pain due to inadequate facilities or incompetent pro-cedures, may be the woman's lot if she is unfortunate enough to fall into the hands of an untrained and unscrupulous abortionist. Because the dangers of illegal abortion have been highly publicized, the woman also lives with the strong fear that she might well die in the process or suffer serious complications afterward. When a relatively competent and safe practitioner is consulted, at least the direct un-pleasantness of the surroundings and the procedures—and probably of the contact with the abortionist himself—will be reduced. But the fear may still persist. Furthermore even the well-intentioned and well-trained abortionist must take steps to protect himself, particu-larly by getting the woman out of his office as soon as possible after the operation. He may also find it necessary to employ various de-vices to preserve his anonymity. There are no substantial data indi-cating the degree to which women are affected by the conspiratorial and secretive nature of the proceedings, but this factor would seem to enhance their general uneasiness and the ambivalence frequently felt about the decision to abort.

Similarly, it is not possible to state with certainty the significance of the woman's knowledge that the behavior in which she is to en-gage is officially designated as "criminal." The fact that millions of women resort to abortion would seem to suggest that the label means little. And it is very likely true that there is "hardly any other section of the criminal law that is so completely out of touch with the feelings of the masses as the law of abortion." [89] On the other hand, lack of deterrent effect does not necessarily imply a total absence of more diffuse influence. As Simone de Beauvoir has noted, "many women are intimidated by a morality that for them retains its prestige even though they are unable to conform to it in their behavior; they inwardly respect the law they transgress, and they suffer from their transgression. . . ."[90] To some extent this ambivalence results from the fact that the decision to abort does represent a thwarting of a natural process of great physiological and psychological significance; it is often said that the aborting woman is conscious of the fact that she is killing something of herself. At the same time, cultural conditioning to the view that abortion is a "crime," together with the objectively sordid conditions under which the illegal abortion is obtained, must be influential in shaping negative feelings. Further research both into cases of strong postabortal guilt and on the attitudes of less severely disturbed women who have had abortions is needed in order to determine the extent to which these negative reactions are "natural" or "cultural." It seems safe to say, though, that any unpleasantness and danger inherent in the termination of pregnancy is enormously increased by the conditions under which most illegal abortions take place.

Religious and Ethical Aspects

Although most Protestant and Jewish spokesmen (with the exception perhaps of extremely Orthodox Jews) appear to uphold the morality of therapeutic abortion—at least as it is presently defined by the law—the Roman Catholic Church's strong doctrinal opposition to all abortion is well-known.[91] Catholic policy forbids even therapeutic abortion, as indicated in the major pronouncement of Pius XI:

As to the "medical and therapeutic indication" to which, using their own words, we have made references, Venerable Brethren, however much we may pity the mother whose health and even life is gravely imperiled in the performance of the duty allotted to her by nature, nevertheless what could ever be a sufficient reason for excusing in any way the direct murder of the innocent? This is precisely what we are dealing with here. Whether inflicted upon the mother or upon the child, it is against the precept of God and the law of nature: "Thou shalt not kill." The life of each is equally sacred, and no one has the power, not even the public authority, to destroy it. It is of no use to appeal to the right of taking away life for here it is a question of the innocent, whereas that right has regard only to the guilty; nor is there here question of defense by bloodshed against an unjust aggressor (for who would call an innocent child an unjust agressor?). Again there is no question here of what is called the "law of extreme necessity" which could even extend to the direct killing of the innocent. Upright and skilled doctors strive most praiseworthily to guard and preserve the lives of both mother and child; on the contrary, those show themselves most unworthy of the noble medical profession who encompass the death of one or the other, through a pretence at practicing medicine or through motives of misguided pity. . . .[92]

Historically, one basis for Catholic objection to abortion has been the belief that the child who dies unbaptized cannot enter Heaven. This has led to various Catholic medical directives prescribing procedures for emergency baptism of the fetus when necessary. Nowadays, however, it appears that the major ground for Catholic policy is simply that emphasized in the statement by Pius XI: the commandment against killing.

The one slight concession to medical necessity appears in the application of the rule of "double effect." Under this doctrine, an act is sometimes construed as having two consequences: one good, one evil. If the act is undertaken in order to attain the good consequence, it is moral, notwithstanding the fact that the evil consequence may also result. In his perceptive discussion of the legal and moral issues connected with abortion, Glanville Williams suggests that extension of this rule of double effect—or "indirect killing," as the variant relating to abortion has been called—might well be relied on to permit therapeutic abortion in many cases of medical necessity.[93]

Thus far, the Church has applied the rule to only a few types of situations. The most recent extension has been to the case of Fallopian pregnancy, in which the fetus grows in a Fallopian tube. In such a case, the death of both mother and child can be predicted if the pregnancy is not terminated. In such a case the Catholic doctor is now permitted to remove the fetus on the ground that this is but an indirect and unintended effect of the necessary removal of the tube.

Restrictions placed on Catholic doctors and nurses are, as Williams points out, a highly significant element in the abortion situation. Whereas the Protestant doctor may follow his individual conscience and best medical judgment, the Catholic doctor is enjoined to adhere to what the Church considers to be theologically sound practice. "Hence arises a lamentable gulf between the practice and attitudes of Catholic and non-Catholic physicians, and the fate of the patient will frequently depend entirely on the religion of her adviser and the denomination of her hospital." [94]

Most medical practitioners who support the practice of therapeutic abortion refuse to accept the assertion that they are upholding immoral action. Their major argument lies in the belief that if a choice between the two must be made, the fetus should be sacrificed and the mother saved. Critics contend that the Catholic position really evades, rather than solves, this problem. There are situations in which the physician sees that it will be possible to save only the fetus *or* the mother. The Catholic doctrine, it has been argued, actually represents a preference for the life of the fetus over that of the mother—despite the fact that presumably the two have equal merit. As Williams points out, this preference may have made sense at a time when the Church stated its opposition to abortion primarily in terms of the importance of baptism, but it is not so convincing now that that argument is no longer central.[95]

This objection to the Catholic stand seems valid even if one grants equal value to the lives of mother and fetus. But many experts would distinguish sharply between the different levels of life involved here, questioning whether abortion really involves killing a human being. Even in theological circles there is debate as to just when "life" begins; but perhaps one need not answer that difficult question to feel that the mother's life should be given preference

when a choice is necessary. As seen earlier, many would extend the
preference to include the mother's health as well as her life.

The moral basis for distinguishing between the levels of life involved is pointed up by the comment of one medical observer regarding attitudes toward abortion in Japan, where the practice is
legal and extremely widespread: "A people who have had the sub-
lime opportunity of experiencing firsthand the full expression of
modern war do not appear too compunctious over the removal of
a few grams of fetal protoplasm from the uterus." [96]

Of course there are other religious and cultural reasons for the
ease with which the Japanese have accepted abortion. Yet critics of
Catholic abortion doctrine have long pointed to the discrepancy
between the Church's position on this subject and its stand on killing in wartime or in self-defense, and on capital punishment. Another moral issue is raised by proponents of therapeutic abortion.
Many consider that the likely adverse impact on such a child of
maternal rejection should be taken into account in weighing the
morality of abortion.

Further arguments against the restrictiveness of the Catholic position combine ethical evaluations with an appreciation of empirical
realities. A crucial point is that, although reliable statistics are not
available, it is well-known that large numbers of Catholic women
do in fact undergo abortions. Religion may well be an important
factor in determining the individual's attitude on this issue, but
degree of religious feeling rather than membership in a particular
religion appears to be the controlling element. The Kinsey project
found that for all religions there was a fairly clear inverse relationship between degree of devoutness and incidence of induced abortion. This was quite pronounced in the figures for Protestants. Although the Catholic and Jewish samples were rather small for
meaningful subdivision in some instances, they revealed the same
general relationship. Thus, in their discussion of abortion among
married women, the researchers report: "The percentage of devout
Catholics with induced abortion experience is extremely low and
[that] of the religiously inactive rather high." [97] As is often noted,
the Church's combined prohibition of abortion and the use of contraceptive devices puts the devout Catholic woman in a peculiarly
difficult position if she is at all desirous of controlling pregnancies.

Whenever Catholic doctrine does deter some Catholic women from obtaining abortions, it may serve a definite function from the Church's standpoint. At the same time, public pressure by the Church for restrictive abortion laws indirectly helps to support the traffic in criminal abortion. To the extent that these laws simply drive many women (Catholic and non-Catholic) from the hospital abortions they desire to the infinitely more perilous and sordid illegal operations the outcome (as a practical matter and not just a doctrinal one) can hardly be viewed as "moral." Furthermore, Catholic doctors and hospitals have been known often to refer abortion-seeking patients to non-Catholic practitioners or facilities. This matter of referral poses an ethical dilemma for all legitimate practitioners. As one writer puts it: "From an ethical standpoint, I see no difference between recommending an abortion and performing it. The moral responsibility is equal." [98] The Catholic doctor's avoidance of direct personal involvement is, in a sense, institutionalized. He can argue and even feel that he has no choice in such a situation; at the same time, he can hardly evade the ethical implications of referring the patient elsewhere.

Policy Alternatives

There has been practically no change in American abortion laws since Taussig wrote, in 1936: "Ostrich-like, we have buried our heads in the sand and refused to look facts in the face." [99] The realization that such laws are ineffectual and may in fact have positively bad effects has created considerable professional support for proposals to widen the legal indications for therapeutic abortion. One approach to abortion reform might be through judicial interpretation of the law. To a certain extent, courts may be hampered by the specificity of statutory directives—as where a law provides an exception only "when necessary to save the life of the mother." However, courts can and do sometimes extend the exception by broadening their interpretation. Thus, in a 1959 California decision, the court held that there is a presumption of necessity when an abortion is performed by a licensed physician, which presumption cannot be overturned merely by showing prior good health. The court also stated:

> Surely, the abortion statute . . . does not mean by the words *unless the same is necessary to preserve her life* that the peril to life be imminent. It ought to be enough that the dangerous condition be potentially present, even though its full development might be delayed to a greater or less extent.[100]

In jurisdictions where the statutory exception extends to "life or health," there are further possibilities for liberalization by judicial decision.

Such action might be objected to, however, as constituting improper "judicial legislation"—that is, as allegedly thwarting the will of the legislature and, indirectly, the will of the people. But in any case it is questionable whether significant short-run change can be effected in this area through judicial action; in the absence of numerous "permissive" decisions, doctors would continue to feel extremely uncertain as to how subsequent cases might be decided. This point is illustrated by the British experience following the well-publicized case of *Rex v. Bourne* in 1938.[101] There, a fourteen-year-old girl had been impregnated as the result of a brutal rape. Bourne, an eminent obstetrician, performed the operation openly in a London hospital, asking no fee and informing the authorities of his action. Charged with unlawfully procuring an abortion in violation of the Offenses Against the Person Act, he was acquitted. Judge McNaghten concluded:

> . . . if the doctor is of opinion, on reasonable grounds and with adequate knowledge, that the probable consequence of the continuance of the pregnancy will be to make the woman a physical or mental wreck, the jury are quite entitled to take the view that the doctor, who, in those circumstances, and in that honest belief, operates, is operating for the purpose of preserving the life of the woman.

Although the broad phrases *probable consequence* and *physical or mental wreck* would seem sufficient to have effected a considerable liberalization of the basis for therapeutic abortion, no new legislation was introduced to formalize this new, liberal basis. As a result,

octors continue to be uncertain as to when abortions would and
would not be "unlawful," very few such operations have been
ranted by hospitals, and illegal abortion continues to flourish much
s before. Of course courts, in America as well as in Britain, can
nfluence abortion policy by refusing to impose stiff sentences in
uch cases, but this does not solve any of the immediate problems
f the woman who is seeking an abortion.

Statutory revision, then, would seem a more hopeful means of
eform. In Great Britain, there has been considerable pressure for
uch reform through the well-organized activities of the Abortion
Law Reform Association—which since 1952 has introduced several
bortion bills into the British parliament. Although no similar or-
anization exists in the United States, various reform proposals
ave been advanced.

The Planned Parenthood Federation's 1955 conference on abor-
ion called for the drafting and eventual adoption of a model abor-
ion law. Drafters of such legislation were urged to recognize the
rowing approval of broadened indications (psychiatric, humani-
arian, and eugenic) for therapeutic abortion, and to consider the
esirability of permitting doctors to give such factors greater weight
1 reaching decisions on applications for abortion.[102]

The American Law Institute, in its Model Penal Code, has now
rafted a model provision which provides in part:

> A licensed physician is justified in terminating a pregnancy if he
> believes there is substantial risk that continuance of the pregnancy
> would gravely imperil the physical or mental health of the mother or
> that the child would be born with grave physical or mental defect,
> or that the pregnancy resulted from rape, incest, or other felonious
> intercourse. All illicit intercourse with a girl below the age of sixteen
> shall be deemed felonious for purposes of this subsection. Justifiable
> abortions shall be performed only in a licensed hospital except in
> case of emergency when hospital facilities are unavailable. . . .[103]

An alternative approach to statutory revision involves primary at-
ntion to, and legal recognition of, the hospital abortion commit-
ee as a control device. Under this proposal, statutory standards for
uch committees would be established, and whenever abortion is
eemed "medically advisable" by a committee adhering to such

standards, all persons involved would be granted immunity fro
criminal prosecution.[104]

OBJECTIONS TO REFORM

It is difficult at present to state definitely what impact su
proposals are going to have, but it seems likely that no widespre
or radical revision of the current restrictive laws can be expect
in the near future. There is, of course, considerable religiously bas
opposition to any proposals for the legalization of abortion. Fu
thermore, there is a belief—at least in some circles—that such 1
form would lead to a vast increase in the abortion rate. It cann
be predicted with assurance just what would happen to the over-a
and illegal abortion rates under limited legalization. There is son
dispute among students of the Scandinavian abortion policies, f
example, as to whether legal permissiveness there has or has n
appreciably reduced the incidence of illegal abortion.[105] It is alwa
possible that, when broad indications for abortion are legally san
tioned, the over-all abortion rate will increase and a substanti
number of illegal abortions will continue to be performed. Non
theless, a vastly increased proportion of abortions would then I
performed under optimum conditions.

Furthermore, liberal abortion legislation may be accompanied
as it is in Sweden, for example—by welfare measures designed
encourage child-rearing. Similarly both Sweden and Denmark ha
established abortion consultation centers, a major aim of which
to convince women not to terminate their pregnancies, and the
is evidence that such efforts are successful in a good many cas
Likewise, widespread free distribution of contraceptive informatic
and devices may be used along with lenient abortion policy, and
is believed by many experts that some day full knowledge and ea
availability of low-cost contraceptive techniques may largely elin
nate the demand for abortions (obviously, however, some types
cases would persist).

It should be noted too that even where there is broad statuto
authorization of abortion, careful administration of the law a
other factors may render unwarranted fears about "opening ti
floodgates." For example, it has been found that the extremely vag

indication "anticipated weakness" (referring essentially to the like-lihood of severe strain in giving birth to and caring for a new child), which was added to the Swedish law in 1946, has been used in only a small proportion of the Swedish applications for abortion. Again, although the Swedish law permits abortion on "humanitarian" grounds where any girl under fifteen is impregnated, some studies suggest that "legal abortion is not used very extensively to prevent illegitimate births in Sweden, at least among young girls." [106] Of course the more lenient attitude toward unwed motherhood in Sweden partly accounts for this latter finding. It is sometimes argued in the United States that liberalization of abortion laws would some-how constitute a sanctioning of "immorality." The suggestion seems to be that proscription of abortion acts as a deterrent to premarital and extramarital relations. Although this may be true in a small number of cases, it is difficult to believe that the possibility of legal abortion would by itself radically alter the sexual behavior of many women. Certainly with the growing knowledge of contraception, which eventually should extend to most social circles in the coun-try, availability of abortion becomes an even less significant factor in influencing sex activity.

Since present abortion laws have clearly failed to curb the un-sanctioned termination of pregnancy, their persistence must be at-tributable to some latent function they serve for society as a whole or for certain groups and individuals. One of the major requisites of a social system is that it adequately maintain its membership. As a result, no society has allowed uncontrolled termination of preg-nancies. In this sense, some control over abortion may be viewed as socially "natural," even if a particular control system is in fact not very effective. It may be also that the members of our society feel some illusory satisfaction in maintaining a formal and ideal stand-ard in this area, even if they are largely unable to conform to it. As Radcliffe-Brown has noted: "The application of any sanction is a direct affirmation of social sentiments by the community and thereby constitutes an important, possibly essential, mechanism for main-taining these sentiments." [107] Perhaps, as in this case, the mere ex-istence of the sanction serves a similar, if diluted, function. It is not even clear, however, just what the normative ideal embodied in present abortion laws represents. If it is primarily a prohibition of

illegitimacy and promiscuity, the situation is greatly confused by
the fact that the law affects more than just illegitimate pregnancies.
One expert has estimated that in the United States nine tenths of
criminal abortions occur among married women with three or more
children, and the same proportion may apply in England also.[108]
If the proscription basically represents a direct prohibition on killing the fetus, then at least there is a certain coherence about the
ideal standard, even though it diverges greatly from actual behavior.
Another factor that definitely seems involved in laws against abortion is the insistence that woman shall not with ease voluntarily
renounce motherhood as a major social role. This could be interpreted as an institutionalized support of the "maternal instinct," a
necessary sex division of labor, or a reinforcement of the subordinate social status of women. Feminists cite woman's right to make
her own decisions regarding the bearing of children as an essential
element of sexual equality. And as Glanville Williams notes: "All
abortion laws have been made by males, and when feminine opinion is tested it is found to be in support of modification." [109]

Summary

Society's disapproval of abortion seems to be related to the need
to perpetuate itself, to the value obtained through professing a
moral ideal even where it is widely contravened in practice, and
to the emphasis on the woman's child-bearing (and, some would
maintain, subordinate) role. The demographic significance of abortion could be explored further through the comparative study of
abortion policies as they relate to other population trends and controls in various specific societies. In the present study, however, the
primary focus has been on how present abortion laws operate in
one particular society, their place in the abortion problem as a
whole, and their meaning for the woman who is seeking an abortion.

The strong demand for termination of unwanted pregnancies
cuts across various social categories. It is voiced not merely by "immoral" women seeking to erase the evidence and results of their

"sin," but also by large numbers of married mothers who, for various reasons, feel unable to carry through their present pregnancies. The legal prohibition on abortion has not significantly stifled this demand. It has, however, inhibited hospitals and individual medical practitioners from performing the operation. Hospitals today do perform some abortions which, according to the strict letter of the law, are illegal (as when the woman has contracted German measles), but generally legal abortions are kept at a minimum. The major result has been to divert abortion-seekers to illegal channels, and to establish the economic base for an illicit traffic in such operations. Criminal abortion has become a highly profitable and well-organized enterprise. Police action against abortionists is, in most instances, impeded by the lack of complainants. Law enforcement authorities must rely on elaborate and intensive surveillance and raiding techniques when they do get a lead, and still face the problem that courts are often unwilling strictly to enforce the abortion laws. Like other criminal activities which flourish because of public demand, the illegal abortion activity has given rise to serious problems of police graft and extortion.

By being forced to resort to illegal facilities, the pregnant woman faces serious dangers which would not be involved in a hospital abortion. She may attempt self-induced abortion, which is either highly ineffective or extremely dangerous. Serious complications, and sometimes even death, may also result from an illegal operation.

An abortion may also have adverse effects on the woman's self-image, although these effects have not been clearly defined. Psychiatrists often cite cases of severe guilt feelings following abortion, but it is not known to what extent these are related to basic psychic contradictions or to cultural conditioning. The fact that the woman is forced to engage in a "criminal" act should not be ignored. In undertaking this type of deviant behavior, the woman usually receives little direct group support. The kind of situation she faces, and the specific treatment she receives, will depend partly on her marital and social status. But in almost all cases hers is in an extremely unpleasant position, one which leaves her vulnerable to various kinds of exploitation.

The futility of attempting to curb abortion by law has led to proposals for more liberal laws aimed at insuring that a substantial proportion of abortions will be properly performed under safe and less demoralizing conditions. Although there is probably only slight support for the proposal to allow abortion merely on socioeconomic grounds, there is strong professional approval for proposals to broaden the psychiatric grounds and to add humanitarian and eugenic indications. The Roman Catholic Church opposes any legalization scheme, but other religious groups appear to accept the medical profession's right to establish criteria for therapeutic abortion. Although no responsible student of the subject approves of abortion as a positive good, many argue that often it is a lesser evil than the sacrificing of the mother's life or health.

Notes

[1] George Devereux, *A Study of Abortion in Primitive Societies* (New York: Julian Press, Inc., 1954), p. 161.

[2] For details of the case see *The New York Times*, July 25, 1962, p. 22; July 27, 1962, p. 12; July 31, 1962, p. 9; and August 1, 1962, p. 19.

[3] Alfred C. Kinsey, in Mary S. Calderone (ed.), *Abortion in the United States* (New York: Paul B. Hoeber, Inc., 1958), p. 55. For more detailed information see Paul H. Gebhard, *et al.*, *Pregnancy, Birth, and Abortion* (New York: Paul B. Hoeber, Inc., 1958), Chap. 4.

[4] Calderone, *op. cit.*, p. 180.

[5] See Edwin M. Schur, "Abortion and the Social System," *Social Problems*, 3 (October 1955), 94-99.

[6] For a fairly recent listing of the various statutory provisions, see Fowler Harper, "Abortion Laws in the United States," Appendix A, in Calderone, *op. cit.*

[7] Herbert L. Packer and Ralph J. Gampell, "Therapeutic Abortion: A Problem in Law and Medicine," *Stanford Law Review*, 11 (May 1959), 418, 419.

[8] Alan F. Guttmacher, "The Shrinking Nonpsychiatric Indications for Therapeutic Abortion," in Harold Rosen (ed.), *Therapeutic Abortion* (New York: Julian Press, Inc., 1954), p. 12.

[9] Christopher Tietze, in Calderone, *op. cit.*, pp. 83, 85.

[10] Packer and Gampell, *op. cit.*, p. 427.

[11] As the Finkbine case suggests, however, a eugenic indication for legal abortion is not always acceptable to the authorities. On the other hand, had there been less publicity in that case and had the hospital performed the operation rather than demand legal clarification, perhaps no significant legal reaction would have resulted.

[12] K. P. Russell, "Therapeutic Abortions in California in 1950," *Western Journal of Surgery, Obstetrics and Gynecology*, 60 (1952), 497.

[13] Tietze, in Calderone, *op. cit.*, pp. 83-84.

[14] Harold Rosen, "The Emotionally Sick Pregnant Patient: Psychiatric Indications and Contraindications to the Interruption of Pregnancy," in Rosen, *op. cit.*, pp. 231, 225.

[15] Howard C. Taylor, Jr., in Calderone, *op. cit.*, p. 108.

[16] Arthur J. Mandy, "Reflections of a Gynecologist," in Rosen, *op. cit.*, p. 295.

[17] Bard Brekke, in Calderone, *op. cit.*, p. 137.

[18] See cases cited by A. F. Guttmacher, "Abortion," in E. S. and W. H. Genné (eds.), *Foundations for Christian Family Policy* (New York: National Council of Churches, 1961), p. 231.

[19] Packer and Gampell, *op. cit.*, pp. 435, 430.

[20] Theodore Lidz and Harold Rosen, in Calderone, *op. cit.*, pp. 95-96, 96.

[21] Alan F. Guttmacher, "Therapeutic Abortion: The Doctor's Dilemma," *Mount Sinai Hospital,* 21 (1954), 111-21, as reprinted in R. C. Donnelly, J. Goldstein, and R. D. Schwartz, *Criminal Law* (New York: The Free Press of Glencoe, Inc., 1962), p. 115.

[22] For the 1950 statistics, see Russell, *op. cit.*, p. 500; the more recent findings are from Packer and Gampell, *op. cit.*, p. 428.

[23] Guttmacher, "Therapeutic Abortion: The Doctor's Dilemma," *op. cit.*, p. 115.

[24] Erving Goffman, "The Medical Model and Mental Hospitalization," in *Asylums* (New York: Doubleday & Company, Inc., 1961), p. 345.

[25] Packer and Gampell, *op. cit.*, p. 429.

[26] Guttmacher, "Therapeutic Abortion: The Doctor's Dilemma," *op. cit.*, p. 116.

[27] See Edwin M. Schur, in Calderone, *op. cit.*, pp. 34-35. The quotation is from *Williams v. U.S.*, 138 F. 2nd 81 (1943).

[28] Gebhard, *et al.*, *op. cit.*, p. 198.

[29] The general New York findings were reported by Carl Erhardt in Calderone, *op. cit.*, pp. 77-78. For the statistics on New York Hospital, see Charles M. McLane, *ibid.*, p. 101.

[30] Mandy, *op. cit.*, pp. 288-289.

[31] Rosen, in Calderone, *op. cit.*, p. 131.

[32] R. E. Watkins, "A Five-Year Study of Abortion," *American Journal of Obstetrics and Gynecology,* 26 (1933), 162; Russell S. Fisher, "Criminal Abortion," *Journal of Criminal Law, Criminology and Police Science,* 42 (July-August 1951), 246.

[33] Gebhard, *et al.*, *op. cit.*, pp. 195-196. For the statistics just cited, see pp. 193-199, and especially Table 71, p. 198.

[34] Louis M. Hellman, and Robert B. Nelson, in Calderone, *op. cit.*, p. 65. The question of death, resulting from induced abortion is considered in later sections of this chapter.

[35] Kinsey, *ibid.*, p. 57.

[36] Abraham Rongy, *Abortion: Legal or Illegal?* (New York: Vanguard Press, 1933), p. 117.

[37] Fisher, *op. cit.*

[38] John Bartlow Martin, "Abortion," *Saturday Evening Post* (May 20, 1961), 19.

[39] Funds and leisure needed for gambling have been mentioned as factors in some cases. Interview with Miss Moira McDermott, Indictments Bureau, and the late Dr. Perry Lichtenstein, Medical Advisor, Office of the District Attorney, New York County, March 31, 1954.

[40] Gebhard, *et al.*, *op. cit.*, pp. 198-199.

[41] G. L. Timanus, in Calderone, *op. cit.*, pp. 62-63.

[42] For an early estimate, see F. J. Taussig, *Abortion, Spontaneous and Induced: Medical and Social Aspects* (St. Louis: The C. V. Mosby Company, 1936). The 1951 figure was given by Fisher, *op. cit.*

[43] Milton Helpern, in Calderone, *op. cit.*, pp. 67-69.

[44] Fisher, *op. cit.*, p. 245.

[45] Interview with McDermott and Lichtenstein, *cit.* The catheter is also sometimes used in attempts at self-induced abortion. For possible results of the inexpert use of the catheter, see the article by Zakin, *et al.*, "Foreign Bodies Lost in the Pelvis During Attempted Abortion with Special Reference to Urethral Catheters," *American Journal of Obstetrics and Gynecology*, 70 (1955), 233. The article deals with seven case studies in which hospital physicians located six catheters and one glass cocktail stirrer.

[46] Iago Galdston, in Calderone, *op cit.*, p. 133.

[47] Guttmacher, in Genné, *op. cit.*, p. 232.

[48] Gebhard, *et al.*, *op. cit.*, pp. 200-202. These fees covered abortions performed only through the 1940's. The study's data show that fees fluctuated with general economic changes, and it can be assumed that current figures would be correspondingly higher.

[49] Martin, *op. cit.*, p. 21.

[50] Jerome Bates, "The Abortion Mill: An Institutional Analysis," *Journal of Criminal Law, Criminology and Police Science*, 45 (July-August 1954), 163.

[51] *Ibid.*, p. 157; see also Jerome Bates and E. S. Zawadzki, *Criminal Abortion: A Study in Medical Sociology* (Springfield, Ill.: Charles C. Thomas, Publisher, 1964), especially Chaps. 4, 6.

[52] *Ibid.*, p. 158.

[53] Rongy, *op. cit.*

[54] *People v. Berger*, 128 Cal. App. 2nd 509, 514; 275 P. 2nd 799 (1954).

[55] Frank Hogan, *Report of the District Attorney County of New York 1946-48* (New York: 1948), p. 125.

[56] Sophia Kleegman, in Calderone, *op. cit.*, p. 113.

[57] Bates, *op. cit.*, p. 164.

[58] Martin, *op. cit.*, Part 2 (May 27, 1961), 52.

[59] Dr. X, as told to Lucy Freeman, *The Abortionist* (New York: Doubleday & Company, Inc., 1962), p. 202.

[60] J. H. Amen, "Some Obstacles to Effective Legal Control of Criminal Abortion," in National Committee on Maternal Health, *The Abortion Problem* (Baltimore: The Williams & Wilkins Co., 1944), p. 123.

[61] Bates, *op. cit.*, p. 166. The same author cites an early estimate that the average operator of a busy mill pays a minimum of $5000 in protection money each year.

[62] R. Fisher, "Criminal Abortion," in Rosen, *op. cit.*, p. 6. After surveying various British reports, one commentator there has concluded that "there is not in England more than one prosecution to every thousand criminal abortions." Glanville Williams, *The Sancitity of Life and the Criminal Law* (New York: Alfred A. Knopf, Inc., 1957), p. 211. As will be seen below, despite one key judicial decision approving broad interpretation of the indications for legal abortion, British policy is generally similar to that of the United States.

[63] See Edwin M. Schur, in Calderone, *op. cit.*, pp. 36-37.

[64] New York has a special immunity statute relating to abortion prosecutions. See New York Penal Law, Sec. 81a.

[65] New York City Sanitary Code, Sec. 90 (1937) .

[66] Hellman, *op. cit.*, p. 42.

[67] *People v. Gallardo*, 41 Cal. 2nd 57, 257 P. 2nd 29 (1953).

[68] The following discussion is based largely on an interview with McDermott and Lichtenstein, *cit.* I have seen no indication in recent reports that the pattern described here would not still be fairly representative of the practice of urban prosecutors. On the use of disguised investigators, see *The New York Times*, April 4, 1951, p. 25.

[69] Williams, *op. cit.*, p. 207.

[70] Edwin H. Sutherland and Donald R. Cressey, *Principles of Criminology*, 6th ed. (New York: J. B. Lippincott Co., 1960), pp. 225-26.

[71] See the general discussion of the Soviet experience in Gebhard, *et al.*, *op. cit.*, pp. 215-18, and primary sources cited therein.

[72] F. J. Taussig, "Effects of Abortion on the General Health and Reproductive Function of the Individual," in National Committee on Maternal Health, *op. cit.*, pp. 39-40.

[73] *The New York Times*, December 1, 1955, p. 9.

[74] Galdston, *op. cit.*, pp. 118, 119, 121.

[75] Helene Deutsch, *The Psychology of Women:* A Psychoanalytic Interpretation (New York: Grune & Stratton, Inc., 1945), Vol. 2, pp. 182, 187.

[76] M. Ekblad, *Induced Abortion on Psychiatric Grounds* (Stockholm: Acta. psychiat. et neurol. scandinav. *Suppl. 99*, 1955), as cited in Gebhard, *et al.*, *op. cit.*, p. 223, and also discussed in Williams, *op. cit.*, pp. 241-45.

[77] K. Malmfors, "The Problem of the Woman Seeking Abortion"; B. Brekke, unpublished paper. Both reported by Brekke, in Calderone, *op. cit.*, pp. 133-35.

[78] The following is based on Gebhard, *et al.*, *op. cit.*, pp. 203-11. See especially Table 74, p. 205.

[79] *Ibid.*, p. 192.

[80] *Ibid.*, p. 162.

[81] *Ibid.*, pp. 180-81.

[82] *Ibid.*, pp. 35-36.

[83] *Ibid.*, pp. 56-57.

[84] *Ibid.*, p. 149.

[85] Deutsch, *op. cit.*, pp. 184-85.

[86] Simone de Beauvoir, *The Second Sex*, translated by H. Parshley (New York: Alfred A. Knopf, Inc., 1957), pp. 491-92.

[87] Flanders Dunbar, "A Psychosomatic Approach to Abortion and the Abortion Habit," in Rosen, *op. cit.*, pp. 27-29.

[88] Lidz, *op. cit.*, p. 127.

[89] Hermann Mannheim, *Criminal Justice and Social Reconstruction* (New York: Oxford University Press, Inc., 1946) , p. 43.

[90] de Beauvoir, *op. cit.*, p. 490.

[91] For some Protestant and Jewish views, see Frank J. Curran, "Religious Implications," and Armond E. Cohen, "A Jewish View Toward Therapeutic Abortion . . ." in Rosen, *op. cit.*, pp. 153-65, 166-74. An excellent discussion of the Catholic position may be found in Williams, *op. cit.*, pp. 192-206. Also generally

relevant on religious attitudes are Joseph Fletcher, *Morals and Medicine* (Boston: Beacon Press, 1960); and Norman St. John-Stevas, *Life, Death and the Law* (Bloomington: Indiana University Press, 1962).

[92] Pius XI, *Casti Connubi* ("On Christian Marriage"). December 31, 1930.

[93] Williams, *op. cit.*, p. 200.

[94] *Ibid.*, p. 205.

[95] *Ibid.*, p. 198.

[96] W. T. Pommerenke, "Abortion in Japan," *Obstetrical and Gynecological Survey*, 10 (1955), 145.

[97] Gebhard, *et al.*, *op. cit.*, p. 115.

[98] Kleegman, *op. cit.*, p. 112.

[99] Taussig, *Abortion, Spontaneous and Induced* . . . , *op. cit.*, p. 396.

[100] *People v. Ballard*, 167 Cal. App. 2nd 803, 335 p. 2nd at 206, as quoted by Zad Leavy and Jerome M. Kummer, "Criminal Abortion: Human Hardship and Unyielding Law," *Southern California Law Review*, 35 (Winter 1962), 139-40.

[101] *Rex. v. Bourne*, 3, All England Reports, 615 (1938). The report is included in Appendix A of Calderone, *op. cit.*, pp. 193-94. On subsequent developments see Eustace Chesser, "The Doctor's Dilemma," *New Statesman* (June 7, 1958), 722.

[102] Calderone, *op. cit.*, p. 183.

[103] American Law Institute, *Model Penal Code*, Proposed Official Draft, Sec. 230.3:2 (Philadelphia: American Law Institute, 1962), pp. 189-90. A subsequent provision requires certification by at least one other physician and submission of such certification to the hospital and (in cases involving felonious intercourse) to the law enforcement authorities.

[104] See Packer and Gampell, *op. cit.*

[105] See various statements in Calderone, *op. cit.*, and the summary of the Swedish experience in Gebhard, *et al.*, *op. cit.*, pp. 221-29.

[106] Gebhard, *et al.*, *op. cit.*, pp. 222, 224-25.

[107] A. R. Radcliffe-Brown, "Social Sanction," in *Encyclopaedia of the Social Sciences* (New York: The Macmillan Company, 1934), Vol. 13, p. 533.

[108] See Williams, *op. cit.*, pp. 224-25, citing estimate by Sophia Kleegman.

[109] *Ibid.*, p. 223. He refers to opinion-poll results in Denmark, Germany, and England.

HOMOSEXUALITY

Theories and Misconceptions

In 1957 a committee of experts appointed to survey the problems of homosexuality and prostitution in Great Britain included among its major recommendations the suggestion that homosexual behavior, between consenting adults in private, should no longer be a criminal offense.[1] Even though this proposal was never enacted into British law, it contributed to a heightened interest in the problem of sexual inversion—in the United States as well as in Britain. A similar recommendation has been included in the American Law Institute's Model Penal Code, and in 1961 Illinois exempted such private acts by consenting adults from that state's statutory prohibitions.

Given the emphasis on public policy adopted in this study, it is quite appropriate that this proposal should be taken as a point of departure in discussing homosexuality as a social problem. One writer recently complained that there has been too much attention to the legal aspects of the subject and not enough to its sociological dimensions.[2] Although such an objection is warranted when fine legal points are considered to the exclusion of sociological aspects, it is worth stressing that patterns of legal definition and control should be of great interest to the sociologist. Such matters are not outside the scope of sociological analysis of deviance; rather, they constitute a key element in such an analysis.

In treating homosexuality as another illustration of crimes without victims, it may be useful to suggest a few of the ways in which it differs from the previously considered problem of abortion.

In the first place, the question of cause has come to take a much more prominent position in analyses of homosexuality. Why an individual becomes a homosexual is viewed as an important question requiring an answer. The abortion-seeking woman, on the other hand, is much less likely to be viewed as sick or even troubled than as a victim of circumstances, a person in a difficult situation.

Then, too, the rationale of restrictive legislation differs in the two cases. The ostensible basis for prohibiting abortion is the wrongness of taking human life; the statutes are aimed at protecting one "person" (i.e., the unborn child) against the damaging act of another (the mother or the abortionist). Antihomosexuality laws, by contrast, are concerned essentially with harm done by a person to himself. *Wrongdoer* and *victim* are the same person in this case; each of the parties to a homosexual act may be viewed by the law as playing both roles simultaneously.

A third area of significant difference concerns the specific consequences of a punitive policy. In the case of abortion, perhaps the most pronounced impact lies in the economic supply-and-demand cycle that repressive law sets in motion and the professionalized (if illicit) supply mechanisms such demand summons forth. As will become evident, the strictly economic aspects are not so pronounced in the case of homosexuality. On the other hand, the problem of exploitation of the deviant is greater and the deviant's self-conceptions come to the fore perhaps even more strongly. Furthermore, the pervasive nature of the deviants' shared problems gives rise to the development of a specialized subculture, quite unlike any bonds that might exist among women seeking abortion.

Thus abortion and homosexuality may be seen as representing somewhat different types of victimless crime situations; drug addiction, to be considered in the next chapter, would represent yet another variant. In all, however, the central element—a willing exchange of desired goods or services—is present, and unenforceability of law and the development of secondary pathology are well in evidence.

DEFINING HOMOSEXUALITY

Although neither the cause (in the narrowest sense) of homosexuality nor its prevalence and distribution need be central concerns in the present discussion, such matters are of evident relevance to public policy, and particularly require some comment because they are subject to widespread misconceptions.

Psychiatrist Robert Lindner has succinctly criticized some widely accepted yet inadequate definitions of homosexuality.[3] As Lindner states, a very popular definition is based on overt appearance and mannerisms—that is, the homosexual is conceived of as a person who looks and acts like a member of the opposite sex. Actually, this is an erroneous notion. Although some homosexuals do adopt some mannerisms typical of the opposite sex, there is no simple correlation between effeminacy and homosexuality or between masculinism and lesbianism. Both scientific studies and informal accounts by participants in homosexual life confirm that the most obvious types comprise but a tiny percentage of all sexual deviants. In fact, blatant displays of effeminacy are viewed with scorn by many male homosexuals; similarly, in some cases it may be an exaggerated display of masculinity that makes one man an object of sexual desire for another. Reporting on some observations of homosexuality in New York City, a journalist recently expressed his strong surprise that so few of the men he saw dancing with one another in "gay (i.e., homosexual) bars "looked" homosexual.[4]

A second misleading definition of homosexuality Lindner describes as "pseudoscientific and statistical." According to this approach, one could examine the sort of data presented in the Kinsey report (for example, cumulative incidence figures for various types of sexual activities) and classify as homosexual those individuals reporting a certain frequency of homosexual activities. Lindner asserts that such statistics confuse "outlet with inclination, activity with psychic tendency." They do not, for example, take into account whether other sexual outlets were available, or whether the activities engaged in were really satisfying to the participants. Lindner concludes that the term *homosexual* should be applied only to "those individuals who more or less chronically feel an urgent sexual desire toward, and a sexual responsiveness to, members of their own sex, and who seek gratification of this desire predominantly with members of their own sex." As he goes on to comment, this definition recognizes inversion as "an attitude basic to the personality wherein it resides, as a compulsion with all the urgency and driving energy that account for its persistence despite the obvious disadvantages of homosexuality as a way of life." [5] The Church of England Moral Welfare Council, in its statement to the Wolfenden Committee, similarly sought to distinguish between isolated homosexual acts and homosexuality as a basic sexual condition or inclination:

> Although most males and females exhibit that decided propensity toward members of the complementary sex which is rightly regarded as normal and natural in human beings, it is incontestable that a minority display an equally marked orientation toward members of the same sex.[6]

Homosexuality, then, can—and often does—take the form of a basic personality orientation rather than a particular type of sexual activity. An alternative definition, suggested by Erving Goffman, would limit the term *homosexual* to "individuals who participate in a special community of understanding wherein members of one's own sex are defined as the most desirable sexual objects, and sociability is energetically organized around the pursuit and entertainment of these objects." [7] This definition has the merit of focusing on a collective or socially structured aspect of the problem which, as will be seen, is extremely important. However, given the possibility that legal policy may significantly reinforce or even indirectly generate the development of such restricted social organization and collective orientations, it would be a mistake to consider such aspects as being necessary elements in all homosexuality.

CAUSAL THEORIES

Just as there are different definitions of homosexuality, there are also highly conflicting explanations of its causes. There have long been attempts to explain homosexuality in terms of "innate" characteristics, but the results of research along these lines have been very unimpressive. According to one recent and careful report, "there is so much evidence on the side of the nurture hypothesis, and so little on the side of the nature hypothesis, that the reliance upon genetic or constitutional determinants to account for the homosexual adaptation is ill founded." [8] It may be worth noting that such "internal" explanations have often been voiced by homosexuals themselves. This may occasionally represent an effort to find some plausible meaning for an otherwise inexplicable compulsion. On the other hand, the value for the deviant in using such statements as a defense against moral blame is obvious.

Today the view is widely accepted that homosexuality constitutes, or at least reflects, some kind of psychological disturbance. The rather vague phrase *some kind of* is used intentionally—for there is wide variation in the particular factors emphasized by different experts. Oral fixation, castration anxiety, and numerous other psychoanalytic and psychological rubrics abound in the professional literature on homosexuality. Psychoanalytic theories tend to emphasize that adult homosexuality is rooted in childhood situations. In reporting on a recent comparison of over 100 homosexual patients with a matched group of nonhomosexual patients, a team of psychotherapists stated: "Our findings point to the homosexual adaptation as an outcome of exposure to highly pathologic parent-child relationships and early life situations." [9] Analysts also stress that homosexuality may represent a fear of the opposite sex as much as a desire for persons of the same sex. Another key element in some explanations of male homosexuality has been the concept of a flight from masculinity, an actual or feared inability to live up to male-role expectations. This concept is expanded, by some of the more sociologically oriented interpreters, to relate male homosexuality generally to changing sex roles in modern Western society—that is, to formulate a structural explanation of the condition, rather than merely to uncover predisposing factors in individual cases.[10]

The psychoanalytic literature suggests that although there may be difficulty in pinning down the exact dynamics underlying any individual case, confirmed homosexuality invariably represents a basic psychosexual orientation—whether or not one chooses to call it a clear-cut disease. The Wolfenden Committee expressed its uneasiness about applying the disease concept to this condition, and indeed a similar approach seems to have been taken by Freud himself in his "Letter to an American Mother":

> Dear Mrs. ———:
> I gather from your letter that your son is a homosexual. . . . Homosexuality is assuredly no advantage, but it is nothing to be ashamed of, no vice, no degradation, it cannot be classified as an illness; we consider it to be a variation of the sexual function produced by a certain arrest of sexual development. . . .
> By asking me if I can help, you mean, I suppose, if I can abolish homosexuality and make normal heterosexuality take its place. The answer is, in a general way, we cannot promise to achieve it. . . . The result of treatment cannot be predicted.
> What analysis can do for your son runs in a different line. If he is unhappy, neurotic, torn by conflicts, inhibited in his social life, analysis may bring him some harmony, peace of mind, full efficiency, whether he remains a homosexual or gets changed. . . .[11]

This statement illustrates the considerable pessimism with which therapists usually approach the matter of conversion. There is definitely no sure and simple cure for homosexuality, and the dominant view is that in most cases therapy at best can only make the patient a better-adjusted homosexual.

Freud's concept of basic human bisexuality, which has since been frequently criticized, complicated the analysis of inversion and has led to such notions as the "homosexual-heterosexual continuum"— accepted by some commentators and utilized in the Kinsey reports. According to these schemes, the individual's *degree* of heterosexuality or homosexuality is determined by measuring his sexual activities and inclinations against those of other individuals. Certain writers have taken the view, also, that the "abnormality" of homosexual behavior is largely a function of adverse value judgments in the society. Cross-cultural and cross-species research has been cited as suggesting that "a biological tendency for inversion of sexual behavior is inherent in most—if not all—mammals, including the human species." [12] A recent psychoanalytic report, however, suggests that such formulations may confuse capacity and tendency; that whereas man may have a capacity for homosexuality, his normal tendency is toward heterosexuality. According to this analysis, homosexuality, far from being either inborn or natural, is "acquired and discovered as a circumventive adaptation for coping with fear of heterosexuality." [13]

Not surprisingly, many homosexuals insist that they are in no sense sick, and several disinterested students of the problem also have questioned the alleged invariable pathology of the homosexual. Thus Lindner has viewed homosexuality as a form of rebellion generated by the conflict between an urgent sexual drive and the repressive measures of conventional sex morality.[14]

Another perspective is offered by Simone de Beauvoir in her discussion of lesbianism. She asserts that homosexuality is "no more a perversion deliberately indulged in than it is a curse of fate. It is an attitude chosen in a certain situation—that is, at once motivated and freely adopted." Refusing to single out any particular type of determining factor as being crucial in individual cases, de Beauvoir states simply: "It is one way, among others, in which woman solves the problems posed by her condition in general, by her erotic situation in particular." [15]

Perhaps even more unorthodox is the view of Albert Ellis. He would go so far as to suggest that under certain circumstances exclusive heterosexuality could be "just as fetichistic" as exclusive homosexuality.[16]

Possible research support for the view that homosexuality need not always be considered psychopathological is found in the work of Evelyn Hooker. She submitted a sample of thirty homosexuals —drawn from the general community, rather than from institutions or private therapy—and a matched sample of heterosexuals to a battery of projective techniques, attitude scales, and intensive life history interviews. When two expert judges examined the test results (knowing nothing about the individual subjects), they experienced great difficulty in distinguishing between matched pairs of homosexual and heterosexual records. Hooker reports that neither judge was able to do better than guess: "In seven pairs both judges were incorrect, that is, identifying the homosexual as the heterosexual, and vice versa; in twelve pairs, correct; and in the remaining eleven they disagreed." (At least half the homosexual cases also were rated as exhibiting high degrees of adjustment.) From such results Hooker concludes that "some homosexuals *may* be very ordinary individuals, indistinguishable, except in sexual pattern, from ordinary individuals who are heterosexual," and that homosexuality, hence, "may be a deviation in sexual pattern which is within the normal range, psychologically." [17]

From a sociological point of view, one would expect that situational elements and learning processes are of importance in causing homosexuality. As noted above, most psychoanalysts stress the significance of family relations in childhood in the formation of such patterns. Beyond that it must be recognized that a homosexual orientation invariably reflects an interpersonal process in which some individuals define others as "homosexual" and react to them accordingly.[18] It is sometimes suggested that seduction is a crucial factor in homosexuality, but it should be realized that most homosexuals have no desire to engage in sexual acts with very young children. Such inclinations are viewed by psychiatrists as symptomatic of a specific and quite different psychic disturbance. As to the apparent seduction of adolescents by adult homosexuals, one must be cautious in appraising the meaning of such activity where it does exist. In the psychiatric research study mentioned earlier, twenty-five homosexual patients and eight control patients claimed to have been homosexually seduced prior to age fourteen. But the researchers comment that "whether an actual sduction took place is open to question, since the burden of guilt and responsibility may have been projected to the partner." They also mention that several of the psychoanalysts reporting cases to the study expressed skepticism about such seduction claims.[19] The writers went on to note that even if the claimed seductions had in fact occurred, that would account for only twenty-five of the 106 homosexual cases; furthermore it would not explain the heterosexual adaptation of the eight heterosexual patients who also had allegedly been seduced.

Every pattern of sexual activity has a starting point. It is all too easy in retrospect to focus on the first incident as causing the later developing pattern. It is also worth keeping in mind that although many heterosexuals are seduced into heterosexuality, seduction is seldom suggested as a cause of their (normal) sexual adaptation.

Prevalence and Distribution

There are no satisfactory statistics regarding the prevalence of homosexuality. The closest approximation to a statistical tabulation is in the Kinsey report data. Projecting from his sample, Kinsey concluded that 4 per cent of adult white males in America are exclusively homosexual throughout their lives after the onset of adolescence, and that 37 per cent of the total male population has had some overt homosexual experience between puberty and old age.[20] Such statistics, as has already been seen, are open to criticism. They are, nevertheless, much to be preferred to haphazard non-empirical estimates which suggest that a vast and powerful homosexual tide may soon engulf the entire country. Such an approach is taken, for example, in a quasisensational (though, in spots, unobjectionable) account, *The Sixth Man*—the title of which derives from the "one out of every six" estimate a homosexual gave to the author.[21]

Although there may well be more homosexuality than the average heterosexual imagines, estimates by individual homosexuals are not likely to be very accurate. Apart from their lack of systematic data, many homosexuals have a psychological stake in exaggerating their number—in order to impress nonhomosexuals that a sizable minority is being mistreated, and in order to bolster their own morale. It is also very difficult to evaluate police figures or other official statistics on homosexuality, fluctuations in which may reflect differentials in law enforcement effort or success every bit as much as they do actual variations in behavior rates.

One point on which all observers are agreed is that official statistics reflect but a fraction of the homosexual behavior that is, in fact, occurring. Most specialists also appear convinced that there has been some increase in homosexuality in recent years—though it is extremely difficult to be sure that such apparent increase is not primarily a reflection of greater research on the problem and more open consideration and discussion of the subject. Kardiner, writing in 1954, found that homosexual patients at that time did, as compared with patients interviewed twenty-five years earlier, report a relatively easier time finding homosexual partners,[22] but even this could reflect an increased openness toward the problem rather than an actual rise in homosexuality. Perhaps the conclusion of the Wolfenden Committee would apply equally well to the American situation—that although the amount of homosexuality might well be "large enough to present a serious problem," such behavior is "practiced by a small minority of the population, and should be seen in proper perspective, neither ignored nor given a disproportionate amount of public attention." [23]

In line with the prevailing misconceptions regarding the appearance and overt behavior of the homosexual (and the corresponding mistaken assumption that homosexuals are easily and quickly identified), there is a widespread belief that most homosexuals are members of a particular social stratum and are engaged in a narrow range of occupations. Research has shown—and homosexuals themselves are quick to confirm—that homosexuality cuts across all boundaries of class and occupation, race and religion.

Although the discussion thus far has related largely to male homosexuality, many of the general points would apply equally well to homosexuality among females. Perhaps even less is known about the prevalence of lesbianism than is known of male homosexuality. The Kinsey investigations uncovered relatively less lesbianism, yet some writers have asserted that there is as much homosexuality among females as among males—or even more. American society holds a relatively casual attitude toward the range of acceptable female attire and mannerisms, and toward the idea of women embracing in public or even living together. Whatever bearing this may have on the existence of female homosexuality, its more general significance is considerable. Lesbians are relatively free to practice their homosexuality, even to the extent of forming more or less permanent homosexual relationships.

Numerous possible reasons have been cited to explain society's greater tolerance of the lesbian. One of the more intriguing is the suggestion of a psychiatrist that "the male ego does not wish to recognize that women could possibly secure sexual satisfaction without the participation of the opposite sex. The tendency for judges not to prosecute [sic] female homosexuals, perhaps, is an unconscious expression of denying its [lesbianism's] existence." [24] Another interesting thesis is set forth in a recent book by two male homosexuals. They note that society generally evaluates maleness more positively than femaleness; hence, the man who acts in an effeminate manner exhibits "weakness," whereas the woman who acts in a masculine manner—in a sense—displays "strength."[25] This view relates nicely to that of Simone de Beauvoir, who sees lesbianism arising, in large measure, as the female's protest against her sex's subordination—an expression of her unwillingness to play the subservient role to the male. Cultural emphasis on female narcissism may also be involved. From this standpoint, a certain amount of lesbianism may be tolerated as the price society pays for encouraging women's constant preoccupation with feminine allure.[26]

The exact meaning of certain characteristics of lesbian behavior is also unclear. For example, lesbian relations seem more affectionate and enduring than those of male homosexuals; there is much less recourse among lesbians to promiscuity and homosexual prostitution, and blackmail of female homosexuals (by sexual partners or non-homosexual exploiters) is rare. Some analysts seem to find in these facts a basis for the relatively tolerant societal reaction. It could be suggested, however, that these characteristics may partly stem from that reaction, rather than produce it.

Laws and Law Enforcement Policies

Although it is not a crime merely to be a homosexual, all American jurisdictions (with the recent exception of Illinois) proscribe homosexual acts—among adults as well as between adults and minors, and in private as well as in public. The homosexual, in other words, has no legal outlet for the kind of sex life to which he is drawn; his only alternative to law-breaking is abstinence. These legal provisions constitute, many observers feel, but one aspect of a more general overabundance of laws governing sexual behavior. Statutes proscribing fornication and laws establishing the crime of "statutory rape" (intercourse between an adult male and a girl below the "age of consent"—even if she does consent) are striking examples of this tendency. Indeed it can be said that all unmarried adolescents and adults in our society—male and female, heterosexually inclined as well as homosexually oriented—are forced to choose between abstinence and "criminality." Although some statutes provide separate definitions of and penalties for particular homosexual offenses, others set forth a vaguely phrased, catch-all offense.[27] Thus the law books are full of such phrases as *unnatural crimes, the infamous crime against nature, any unnatural copulation, the abominable and detestable crime against nature with mankind or beast, unnatural intercourse,* and *any unnatural and lascivious act.* These terms obviously reflect an attitude of moral condemnation; they do not display the degree of specificity usually required in the statutory definition of crimes.

The penalties theoretically imposable for homosexual acts are harsh ones. Quite a few states, for example, provide a maximum penalty (for some homosexual offenses) of ten or more years in prison. Since 1951 at least six states have reduced penalties in this area; on the other hand, during the same period several states have increased the maximum sentences for certain homosexual offenses. The tremendous variation in statutory definitions and prescribed penalties in the different jurisdictions has been described as "chaotic." [28] Judge Morris Ploscowe has stressed the incongruities resulting from this statutory variation:

> [Penalties can range] from one-year maximum in New York for a crime against nature with the consent of a person over eighteen years of age, to life imprisonment in Nevada. Delaware and Virginia decree a maximum of three years' imprisonment for this offense. On the other hand, the maximum in Connecticut is thirty years. Four states—Louisiana, New Hampshire, New Jersey, and Wisconsin—provide a five-year *maximum* for sodomy. In four other states—Montana, Idaho, Arizona and Tennessee—however, five years is the *minimum* for this offense.[29]

In some jurisdictions the homosexual may also be subject to long-term incarceration, ostensibly for treatment, under special "sex offender" or "sexual psychopath" laws. These laws—which establish an extremely vague "waste-basket" category of offenders and allow for commitment with less than the usual criminal law safeguards—are often applied against minor sex offenders, and not just as a means of isolating dangerous sex criminals.

Of course, statutory possibilities alone do not provide a realistic picture of the homosexual's legal status. The attitudes of judges and juries are of considerable importance, and—although these tend to vary greatly—there does seem to be a reluctance (in the absence of the use of force, the involvement of a minor, or participation in blatantly inappropriate public display) to impose stringent sanctions against homosexual defendants. For many inverts, however, the exposure involved in arrest and trial may be almost as damaging as actual conviction. As Peter Wildeblood stated, with reference to his own case: "I felt that it did not much matter what the verdict might be; it was a trial by smear, not a trial by jury, which I was about to undergo." [30]

ENFORCEMENT TACTICS

It is safe to say, though, that the average homosexual does not face a strong likelihood of harsh punishment at the hands of the law. This so primarily because of the tremendous difficulties the police face in seeking to enforce these laws, and the attitudes they consequently adopt. Here again is seen, as in the case of abortion, the significance that the problem of obtaining evidence holds in relation to control of deviance. Because there is a willing exchange of services involved, there is no complainant—except, occasionally, in instances when force has been used, an indecent assault on a nonhomosexual has been made, or a blatant public display has taken place. When the behavior occurs in relative privacy, it usually does not even become known to law enforcement authorities. As a result, the police are placed in an intolerable position. Under great pressure from some segments of the public to eradicate the offending behavior, and at the same time knowing full well the essential unenforceability of this type of law, law enforcement officers fall back on an amalgam of unsavory vice-squad techniques and "looking the other way." In the large cities, there tend to be fairly routine patrols of public places frequented by homosexuals, with intermittent arrests made in those situations viewed as being most offensive to the public at large.

The typical technique for effecting arrest involves the use of plainclothes detectives as decoys to draw indecent proposals; these proposals then provide the evidence against the offender. As a British police expert has stated:

> . . . the term *agents provocateurs* is a justly pejorative name for young police decoys, whose squalid hunting ground is the public urinal. . . . I should have thought it apparent that the time had now come to discontinue this miserable stratagem in importuning cases, rather than go on denying that it exists. If the importuning is as difficult to detect as all that, it can't matter much to "public decency." [31]

Apart from the possible danger that otherwise innocent bystanders could be trapped into compromising statements, such spy techniques may be viewed as abhorrent to the democratic way of life. The police sometimes argue that such techniques represent the only way of enforcing the existing laws—a statement that can be used as an argument for statutory reform. Some protection against abuse is afforded by the legal doctrine of entrapment (under which police decoy practices are sometimes ruled improper), and at least one important federal court decision reversed a conviction based on the uncorroborated testimony of the arresting officer where the evidence as to actual guilt was equivocal. Pointing to the severe nature of the accusation and the varying possibilities for others to exploit it for their own gain, the court stated:

> Any citizen who answers a stranger's inquiry as to direction, or time, or a request for a dime or a match is liable to be threatened with an accusation of this sort. There is virtually no protection, except one's reputation and appearance of credibility, against an uncorroborated charge of this sort. At the same time, the results of the accusation itself are devastating to the accused. . . . The gratuitous solicitation of a total stranger for a perverted act is a phenomenon on the outer fringes of behavior . . . in the practical world of everyday living it is a major accusation. . . .
> . . . the testimony of a single witness to a verbal invitation to

sodomy should be received and considered with great caution. The great public interest that charges of this offense be not preferred without solid foundation requires that there be a known strictness on the part of the courts which will serve to deter prosecutors in dubious cases.[32]

Law enforcement activity is also directed at such known homosexual meeting places as "gay" bars. Plainclothesmen are often stationed as decoys in such establishments, operating in a fashion similar to that adopted in public parks and toilets. But legal action is also periodically taken against the bars themselves. The legal basis for this action varies—it may be a special statute or ordinance, or the general prohibition against "disorderly conduct" or conduct "contrary to public welfare or morals." State liquor authorities have been particularly active in this regard.

The judicial decisions in such cases have been conflicting. Whereas the authorities may have no difficulty in closing down an establishment if they provide proof of actual illegal or immoral acts on the premises, their position may be less certain if they merely establish the nature of the bar's general reputation and clientele.[33] Actually, the policy toward homosexual bars seems to be one of regulation and irregular harassment, rather than one of full-fledged opposition aimed at eventual elimination. Although the threat of official action is always present—and may give rise to "a complex system of graft, bribery, payoffs, corruption, and underworld skulduggery" [34]—it does not seriously interfere with ongoing activities. A report from New York states: "A police cruiser was parked in front of one of the dancing bars I visited and its driver was standing inside the door talking to the proprietor as I entered, but no one in the back room, where about twenty-five male couples were dancing, paid any notice to this." [35]

The typical over-all law enforcement policy on homosexuality, then, appears to be a fairly pragmatic one. Police realize that they must, to a certain extent, adopt a live-and-let-live outlook. They act as vigorously as possible in cases involving force or minors; furthermore, public outrage over any type of sex crime may be an occasion for stepped-up activity against known homosexuals and their gathering places. Although some law enforcement personnel certainly harbor sadistic attitudes toward homosexuals, today such attitudes may not be widespread. A handbook for plainclothesmen notes:

> In recent years the terms *fag, fairy,* and *queer* have fallen into the discard [*sic*] in law enforcement circles. The general term *degenerate* has had the same fate. The homosexual is now called a *sex deviate,* and *degenerate* is now used as a term to describe the more bestial molester of women or children.[36]

Admittedly, the labels in themselves provide no reliable indication of attitude, yet this change seems to reflect more than a trend toward euphemisms. Even if the police do not engage in continual and all-out persecution of homosexuals, however, it may be questioned (given the relatively meager results) whether the use of policemen as decoys and for other surveillance of homosexuals is justified—particularly when there are more urgent social problems to which such efforts might be directed.

Patterns of Exploitation

The homosexual, although the danger of direct police action is not overwhelming, must be constantly aware of his precarious position vis-à-vis the law, and of the fact that he himself has little recourse to the law should such need arise. As a result he finds himself highly vulnerable to exploitation, by the police as well as by others. This vulnerability manifests itself particularly in the danger of blackmail, often cited in discussions of homosexuality. There is little doubt that the law, as it now stands, encourages the blackmail of homosexuals. In a House of Lords debate in 1954, The Right Honorable the Earl of Jowitt remarked that, during his term as attorney-general, "at least 95 per cent of the cases of blackmail which came to my knowledge arose out of homosexuality." [37] There is every reason to believe that this situation is at least as bad today, and that such an assessment may apply as readily to the United States as to Britain.

The technique may be informal or quite elaborate, the individual act of a male prostitute or other delinquent or the carefully planned system of professional criminals. Professional thieves have long been aware of the potentialities of the shakedown, a particular form of which (the "muzzle"—described below) has been applied to homosexuals since the early 1900's. "Arrests are so rare that when one does occur it is a matter for much discussion among thieves. In order to complain to the police, the victim would admit his part in the action, and few will do that." [38] Such shakedown operations can be extremely well organized, with a supposedly homosexual "steerer" luring the victim into a compromising situation and with other participants pretending to be policemen. These activities have proved highly lucrative; there are numerous instances on record of individuals paying out thousands of dollars in extortion money.

His lack of recourse to the law, which makes him vulnerable to blackmail, also leaves the homosexual prey to theft and violence. Indeed there has developed in recent years a fairly distinct subcultural pattern of delinquents dedicated to "baiting queers" and "rolling queers." Although some law enforcement authorities insist that homosexuals should report all exploitation to them, most homosexuals are unlikely to find this advice very reassuring. Certainly enlightened enforcement officers are more interested in catching extortionists than in persecuting inverts. Yet the fact that some police officers have themselves victimized homosexuals is enough to make the latter wary. The payoffs by proprietors of "gay" bars represent an indirect form of exploitation, but sometimes a more direct approach is used. In fact, one writer asserts: "There are such large numbers of corrupt policemen who victimize homosexuals that some law enforcement agencies actually have secret members entrusted with the task of discovering extortion practiced by the officers of the law." [39] It is not difficult to see why the police officer may be tempted into such practices. The strong public disapproval believed to attach to homosexuality, the extreme reluctance of homosexuals to report victimization (particularly at the hands of the police), and the discretion the officer may exercise in deciding when homosexual behavior is an "offense," all serve as inducements.

The homosexual's lack of legal status has been further impressed upon him by various rulings stating that he is ineligible for service in the armed forces and employment in other government agencies. A valid argument may be presented regarding the undesirability of placing homosexuals in the all-male military setting. More difficult to defend is their dismissal from military service with less than honorable discharges and their exclusion from benefits under the GI Bill of Rights after they have actually served. With regard to other government employment, two reasons have been given for the dismissal of homosexuals: their general (moral) unsuitability, and their peculiar susceptibility to blackmail (which is believed to constitute a security risk).

The preconceptions of the Senate subcommittee that investigated this matter are indicated by its listing among its primary objectives an intention "to consider why [not *whether*] their employment by the Government is undesirable. . . ." As to general unsuitability, the subcommittee referred to the importance of "acceptable standards of personal conduct"; yet it did not develop clearly the reasons for singling out this particular form of unacceptable or immoral conduct as requiring a special personnel policy.[40] The allegation that homosexuals pose security risks may have more validity. As has already been suggested, homosexuals do seem highly vulnerable to blackmail. It is true, as Goffman has pointed out, that any person in possession of a "discreditable secret" may be subject to such exploitation.[41] As the recent Profumo-Keeler scandal in Britain and other such incidents suggest, heterosexual as well as homosexual behavior can easily establish a basis for extortion. Nevertheless, although circumstances will vary greatly in particular cases, there is probably reason to believe that the imputation of homosexuality (in cases where the condition has hitherto been successfully hidden) is more damaging than many other possible types of personal discrediting. The combination of threats to legal status, to occupational and economic security, to various interpersonal solidarities, and to an often-precarious management of major personal identity problems is a formidable one. Homosexuals themselves seem to argue both ways on the issue of their vulnerability to blackmail. On the one hand, they describe at length their victimization by extortionists. On the other hand, in claiming that the security-risk label is unjustified, they insist they are no more susceptible to blackmail than other persons are. It is unlikely that both these positions can be maintained simultaneously. What can be said, however, is that the societal reaction to homosexuality (including labeling them as "security risks") itself actively promotes the discreditability of the homosexual. Thus the government's claim of easy blackmail is self-confirming.

The Homosexual Community

Although legal stigmatization and harassment make the homosexual's life difficult, they rarely push him into a life of sexual abstinence. Often, however, such pressures do significantly color his sexual and social relationships. An important aspect of the problem of homosexuality in our society is the development of a special homosexual subculture—not merely the gathering together of homosexuals, but a more general culture-within-a-culture, with its distinctive values and behavior norms, modes of speech and dress, as well as its special patterns of interaction and social differentiation. To the extent that a homosexual immerses himself in this subculture, he must undergo a particular socialization process. Homosexual inclination, at least where it is exclusive, may reflect a basic personality orientation. But living as a homosexual, in the sense of the Goffman definition cited earlier, involves the learning of a special social role. This element is suggested by the phrase *coming out,* which is used among homosexuals to refer to "one's recognition of oneself as a homosexual or one's entrance into the ongoing stream of homosexual life, specifically into the bar system and the privately organized social affairs." [42]

Albert Cohen has written: "The crucial condition for the emergence of new cultural forms is the existence, in effective interaction with one another, of a number of actors with similar problems of adjustment." [43] If this is so, it is easy to see why homosexuals develop a subculture, whereas some other types of deviants (such as women who have illegal abortions) do not. Homosexuality is a continuing orientation, not merely an isolated act. The homosexual shares with similarly inclined individuals significant problems of adjustment—some would probably exist under any sociolegal status, others are created by the pressures directed against homosexuals. Above all, it is the very nature of their particular deviance for homosexuals to be drawn into interaction with one another. The "services" the homosexual demands can, it is true, sometimes be provided by nonhomosexuals, but this will not always be a fully satisfactory solution. In any case, the homosexual *can* find a solution among like-minded individuals in a way the abortion-seeking woman cannot. The homosexual is, in a sense, the source of supply as well as the locus of demand.[44] This is why legal proscription does not lead to a pronounced development of professionalized illicit traffic in homosexuality, as it does in the case of abortion. It is partly this particular type of supply-demand nexus, then, that generates the homosexual community.

GATHERING PLACES

One important feature of homosexual life is the congeries of "gay" bars and other establishments which cater—exclusively or mainly—to homosexuals and which now exist in most large American cities. Given our society's disapproval of any public manifestation of homosexual inclination or behavior, it is not at all surprising that homosexuals have sought out (and the larger society has encouraged) special places in which to congregate. Such establishments, of course, serve the very important function of providing a meeting place at which sexual contacts may be initiated. But they also serve the vital function of enhancing group cohesion and morale in the face of persistent moral condemnation by the society as a whole. For the individual homosexual, such places provide a much-needed opportunity to drop the mask he is often obliged to wear in the "straight" (nonhomosexual) world.

For the individual living a double life—and it should be emphasized that probably most homosexuals pass as heterosexual in much of their social interaction—there must be a spatial as well as behavioral division of his two worlds. These special establishments are "back places, where persons of the individual's kind stand exposed and find they need not try to conceal their stigma, nor be overly concerned with cooperatively trying to disattend it."[45] The homosexual, an outsider everywhere else, is here the insider and may even be able in this setting to subject nonhomosexual interlopers to extreme discomfort—that is, to "a status-degradation ceremony, with the outsider as the denounced participant." [46] Yet even here the homosexual is not entirely at ease: he runs the slight risk of a chance encounter with someone from his other "world," and he is not completely free of legal interference.

Although such establishments are sometimes condemned as breeding grounds of homosexuality, the charge is not convincing. Most of the people who go there (apart from tourists and some "straight" friends) already are involved in the homosexual life. Anyone who wanders in and who is offended by what he sees is perfectly free to leave. The authors of a recent "view from within" emphasize that although an increase in homosexuality may increase the demand for homosexual bars, the bars can scarcely be said to produce homosexuals. Indeed, as these writers go on to suggest, the bars serve to keep homosexuals "in their place"—out of more public places and, to a certain extent, beyond the public view. [47]

It is difficult to say to what extent such establishments have been generated by antihomosexual pressures. It is very likely that homosexuals would want to gather together anyway, though were they more accepted by the larger society such bars might not play so dominant a role in their organized life. It is true that there are persons who benefit economically from such enterprises, but the nature and extent of these benefits do not seem to merit the designation "illicit market"—such as would be used in describing the supply of illegal abortion services or drugs. Of course a crucial point is that, notwithstanding occasional legal harassment, the service provided in this instance is, in itself, a legal one.

There are other types of establishments also catering to homosexuals. Some coffeehouses and Turkish baths have come to be recognized gathering places, and—according to recent reports—certain gymnasiums draw a predominantly homosexual clientele from among that group of inverts who are attracted by and dedicated to a kind of overcompensated masculinity. As is well-known, particular beaches, sections of parks, and street corners may also be frequented by homosexuals—and certain localities may even become homosexual centers (as part of Fire Island, New York, is reputed to be). One writer refers to a number of clothing stores, restaurants, barbershops, tailors, and even some stationers (who "carry a line of greeting cards for 'gay occasions' "), all in New York City, but he goes on to make this comment: "Some homosexuals feel enough group loyalty to patronize mainly those establishments considered 'gay,' usually because of their employees, but others are indifferent to the point of calling them 'fruitstands.' " [48] These references are not intended to suggest either an extensive web of homosexual activities or any kind of conspiracy to take over particular businesses or neighborhoods—as has been hinted at or directly alleged in some of the less responsible journalistic treatments of homosexuality. On the other hand, it is noteworthy that when such deviants are not permitted to mix freely and openly with the general public, alternative institutions do develop.

HOMOSEXUAL RELATIONSHIPS

In all this, the need most homosexuals feel in much of their everyday existence to pass for normal, and constantly to guard against any exposure of their "discreditable secret" features significantly. This same factor significantly affects the nature of homosexual encounters. It is generally noted that most sexual relationships among inverts are short-lived and relatively anonymous and that homosexuals are, correspondingly, highly promiscuous. Homosexual "marriages" do exist, and some have been known to last for many years, but such an arrangement is clearly the exception rather than the rule. It is not difficult to see why this should be so. Public suspicion of adult males who "set up house" together runs high, and for homosexuals who attempt to "pass" (in, say, the occupational sphere) an arrangement of this sort is likely to create new problems. Furthermore, there is really nothing to prevent or make difficult a break in the relationship. The elements of security, status, and children, which help to strengthen the bonds of heterosexual marriage, are absent. And whereas a supportive ideology operates to counteract divisive tendencies in normal marriage and to impel the partners to avoid disruption at almost all costs, a homosexual couple is unlikely to feel any such compulsion.

Most homosexuals claim to be seeking love in their sexual relationships, or at least to view this as an ideal. Yet they express some uncertainty as to whether permanent relationships, even under better conditions, would always be the preferred pattern. Cory and LeRoy claim for example, that because the bearing and rearing of children is a crucial function of normal family life, even a permanent (socially accepted) homosexual union would be bound to fall short of the full attainments of a real marriage. Indeed, they suggest, in his search for sex and companionship the homosexual may be mistaken even in seeking to imitate the heterosexual ideal.[49] At least, then, the homosexual cannot expect from a serious relationship all the satisfactions of normal family life. Suggestions that homosexual couples be permitted to adopt children have been seriously advanced, but it seems clear that this would run so strongly counter to existing norms as to be totally unacceptable.

Not only are permanent relationships infrequent, but even less lengthy affectional-sexual links tend to be overshadowed in homosexual life by the predominant pattern of "cruising" and relatively impersonal one-night stands. (A roughly comparable situation in heterosexual life would arise if most sexual intercourse occurred on blind dates.) Again, there may be various explanations of this phenomenon. An interesting point reported in one study was that among homosexual acquaintances there may sometimes be an informal prohibition on sexual relationships within the primary group "in a manner suggestive of the incest taboo"; this, in turn, drives the members outside their own circle to the known homosexual meetingplaces in search of sexual partners.[50] But all accounts agree that at least one important factor promoting the one-night stand is the "problem of evading social controls" that almost all homosexuals face in one degree or another.

The Homosexual Prostitute

In this pattern of one-time sexual encounters, the homosexual prostitute plays a significant role, providing services which—for one reason or another—a homosexual cannot or does not wish to obtain freely and anonymously elsewhere. The image of aggressive masculinity projected by the prostitute may genuinely attract some homosexuals, who for that reason—and perhaps also because the increased sordidness of the encounter fits their personality needs—actually prefer contact with the hustler (as homosexual prostitutes are called) to a less exploitative relationship. The older and less attractive homosexuals are especially likely to need the hustler—youthfulness and physical attractiveness being highly valued in the homosexual life. Married homosexuals from out of town and ultrasecretive homosexuals who seek the ultimate in anonymity may also be among the hustler's customers. Another possibility is that the hustler will be "kept" by a wealthy customer. Such an arrangement may sometimes enhance the benefactor's status; it may also bring considerable material benefit to the hustler. Frequently the hustler exploits such an arrangement for all it's worth, notwithstanding any beneficent or friendly motives activating the other partner.[51]

There is also as in heterosexual prostitution a sense in which the customer may feel superior by virtue of his ability to buy the other's services. Hustlers seek to offset this humiliation by a contemptuous attitude toward their clients and by "making them pay"—not only in direct fees, but also through frequent robbings and beatings.

There appear to be at least two major types of prostitutes: hustling delinquents who do not conceive of their activity as a career, but simply view the homosexual as fair game, and hustling as another way to make money; and male prostitutes who are definitely oriented to hustling as a career.[52] Both types typically insist they are not themselves homosexual, and seek to regulate their behavior with customers in such a way as to sustain this impression. Thus the relationship (or more accurately, the act) is strictly impersonal—a commercial transaction. The customer gets only what he pays for, and the hustler, as businessman, obtains no sexual satisfaction (or at least seeks to convey that impression). The hustler also may limit himself to those particular varieties of sexual act that he finds least humiliating—typically those popularly considered more masculine (what some accounts term the "active" as distinguished from the "passive" role). Notwithstanding these attempts to insulate themselves from the imputation of homosexuality, it is widely believed that most—if not all—hustlers do have strong homosexual tendencies. Thus, two knowledgeable writers insist that "these hustlers *do* enjoy their homosexual encounters" and that their professed contempt for the customers often "is actually projected self-hatred." And they note: "In 'gay' circles there is a proverb which states: 'Today's trade [i.e., professed nonhomosexuals willing to engage in homosexual acts] is tomorrow's competition.' " [53]

Whatever the psychological makeup of these individuals may be, there is no doubt that the role of hustler has become a well-institutionalized element in homosexual life. In speech, clothing, gesture, and other behavior, the hustler adopts the standardized model demanded by the situation.[54] As several researchers have pointed out, most hustlers are not "seduced" into this activity by confirmed homosexuals; on the contrary, the prospective hustler usually learns about it from his peers, and then takes up the role, knowing quite well what is involved.

Some amount of homosexual prostitution could probably be anticipated even under a less punitive approach to homosexuality. On the other hand, were concealment not a major preoccupation of homosexuals, one might expect a reduction in such practices. Given the impersonal, mutually exploitative, contemptuous, and hasty nature of these encounters, it is extremely unlikely that they are highly satisfying to many individuals. Even if homosexuals exhibit some personality obstacles to uniting affectional and sexual impulses (as some psychiatrists suggest), free and at least friendly modes of sexual expression would seem preferable, from the invert's standpoint if not from that of society as well.

Status and Occupation

Immersion in the homosexual subculture does not render the homosexual immune from social influences emanating from the larger social order. Even if *homosexual* becomes a major status and role for those who are "in the life," it is not the only one. Such persons will most likely have to interact or be placed according to "straight" standards in some significant spheres of their nonsexual behavior. For instance, the Negro homosexual is a Negro as well as a homosexual; the homosexual lawyer cannot restrict his behavior and identity to that which centers on his sexual orientation.

Homosexuals sometimes assert that race and social class are of no significance in the "gay" world. Of course it is true that a person in any social group or category may, in his early years, be subjected to conditions which generate an exclusive homosexual orientation. This does not mean, however, that the respectable society's status order has no acceptance in homosexual life. It has been noted that Negroes often seem quite acceptable to whites as homosexual partners: "even many white homosexuals who will not accept Negroes socially nonetheless are 'quite democratic in bed.' " [55] That such behavior implies equal acceptance of the Negro is anything but clear; in fact, the statement just quoted suggests the opposite. What may often happen is that a Negro exploits his homosexuality (or his willingness to engage in such behavior even if not a confirmed homosexual) for social advantage he could not otherwise maintain, while the white homosexual exploits the Negro's low social status for sexual advantage. Hustling, and even being "kept" by a homosexual, may sometimes be a last resort for the destitute Negro (or white) who cannot obtain other work, or for the alienated who may be contemptuous of ordinary work—"a few beat men hustle themselves a couple of nights a week in uptown homosexual bars, making enough money to stay straight in the Village the rest of the week. . . ." [56] Undoubtedly some white homosexuals are genuinely tolerant, but others may actually be engaging in exploitation while professing their freedom from racial snobbery.

It is likewise frequently reported that homosexual encounters cut across lines of socioeconomic status. This is undoubtedly true—particularly as regards contacts with male prostitutes. But, again, it is unlikely that the reason for this freedom is status tolerance, or that it always leads to a significant reduction of social distance between partners of different class positions. As has been seen, an exogamous rule may cause the homosexual to seek sexual partners outside his own circle of homosexual acquaintances. Because greater social distance implies increased anonymity, and because in any case the proportion of lower-class members is probably greater among hustlers than among homosexuals generally, it stands to reason that a good deal of interclass contact will occur. The situation of a lower-class hustler and a middle-class homosexual engaged in sexual behavior may nicely illustrate the point that a primary group and a primary relationship are two different things. There need have been no tolerance of different statuses for the encounter to take place and there need be no likelihood that social intimacy or identity of viewpoints will result.

In this respect, the transaction is similar to that found in heterosexual prostitution—which would hardly be cited as showing the customers' tolerance of lower-status persons. Much of the same reasoning could also be applied to many of the noncommercial homosexual one-night stands; preservation of anonymity and accessibility of partners are the governing factors, not social tolerance. It is also noteworthy that, according to several reports, status differences and a status hierarchy within the homosexual community are recognized by many homosexuals. This would at least be true with regard to circles of acquaintanceship and preferred meeting places, even if not to all sexual encounters.[57]

Although it is well-known that some occupations provide greater acceptance of sex deviance than others, it must be emphasized that every occupational category probably includes some homosexuals. The situation relating to those particular occupations which tend, in our society, to be defined as relatively effeminate, is a complicated one. It could be argued that men of homosexual inclination are "naturally" drawn to these occupations—or, alternatively, that anyone seeking such work with knowledge of the prevailing social definitions must tend toward a homosexual orientation. On the other hand, it seems indisputable that anyone becoming interested in these fields, whatever the reason, will face a strong likelihood of being socially defined as effeminate. A boy who at an early age develops a predominant interest in ballet dancing is probably going to experience considerable difficulty in sustaining a masculine self-image. For whatever reason, it is in fact now probable that there is a higher proportion of revealed homosexuality in certain job categories—such as interior decoration, ballet and chorus dancing, hairdressing, and fashion design—than in others. The adjective *revealed* is important, because the true proportions for those occupations in which greater concealment is necessary are not known. It has been suggested that the extent to which homosexuality is tolerated in his particular occupation is probably the major factor determining whether an invert will maintain a secret or an overt adaptation. Relatively tolerant occupations include those that "have traditionally accepted homosexual linkages in the popular image" (such as the ones just mentioned); there may also be considerable tolerance in certain low-status jobs (counterman and bellhop have been cited as examples). For their sample of twenty-five secret and fifteen overt homosexuals, Leznoff and Westley found a relationship between type of adaptation and occupation: "The overt homosexual tends to fit into an occupation of low status rank; the secret homosexual into an occupation with a relatively high status rank." [58] In any case, it is quite clear that undisguised homosexuality is at present considered incompatible with many types of work in the business world and in the traditional professions. As Becker has pointed out, the pressures on such deviants may not even be fully met by successful concealment—as when the homosexual encounters the expectation (sometimes a prerequisite for occupational success) that he marry or demonstrate heterosexual prowess one way or another.[59]

It must be re-emphasized that the homosexual invariably must come to grips with the larger society. With rare exceptions, he faces the ever-present possibility (if not acute threat) of police action. In most instances there will be some spheres of interaction in which he finds it necessary to conceal his condition. Even those homosexuals who do not attempt concealment cannot avoid all contact with heterosexual individuals and values; on the contrary, they continually experience the sting of society's disgust and derision. It is hardly surprising, then, if homosexuals seek to carve out a social and even territorial niche within which they can interact largely with their own kind. As Goffman notes, those who share a deviant's stigma are singularly equipped to provide him "with instruction in the tricks of the trade and with a circle of lament to which he can withdraw for moral support and for the comfort of feeling at home, at ease, accepted as a person who really is like any other normal person." [60] The "tricks of the trade" and an entire "way of life" have arisen as a result both of the imperatives of the homosexual condition and the social and legal pressures driving homosexuals into back places.

Homosexuals: A Minority Group?

Discussions of the problem of homosexuality sometimes suggest an analogy to the position of racial and ethnic minority groups. Although such a view could be dismissed as having obvious value to the homosexual apologist, it is difficult to overlook the close similarities that do exist—the pejorative labels, the stereotyped humor, and the relative tolerance in particular occupations. The sexual deviant faces some of the same pressures encountered by the minority group member. He has open to him roughly the same directions of adaptation—assimilation through "passing," accommodation, or militant conflict. From the standpoint of societal regulation of minority-majority relations, it can be seen that a policy of fairly rigid subcultural and occupation segregation is in force in the case of homosexuality. The public may complain about the "gay" bars and about the congregation of homosexuals at certain parks or beaches, and writers may express alarm about the "take-over" of particular occupations by homosexuals. But in fact this segregation proves highly functional for the dominant majority. In homosexuals, as Cory has suggested, society "finds itself with a group of people who cannot be assimilated, cannot be wiped out, and cannot be recognized." [61]

Homosexuals have not all accepted the decision of society that they shall remain segregated. Many homosexuals do pass for normal; this, however, does not disrupt the segregative mechanisms—it actually supports them. At the same time, the individual involved surrenders his chances for militancy and succumbs to the dominant norms. Some homosexuals have chosen the path of militant opposition, which often must take collective form. The homosexual lawyer, for example, could conceivably refuse to practice concealment, but the consequences would simply be loss of job and—probably—disbarment. By banding together in formal action organizations, homosexuals may see some slight hope of influencing the over-all course of events to their advantage. Thus there has arisen what is sometimes called "the homophile movement," comprising organizations that seek to create better understanding of the homosexual, to work for legal reform, to aid homosexuals in trouble with the law, and to help homosexuals themselves (through group discussions and organization publications) come to grips with their own problems. These organizations reportedly exist in many countries; hence, there has been some tendency to speak of a "worldwide" social movement. Such terminology appears, however, to exaggerate both the size and the influence of such groups.[62]

HOMOSEXUAL ORGANIZATIONS

In the United States, there are several of these homophile organizations. The most active are The Mattachine Society and One, Inc., which emphasize the problems of the male homosexual, and the Daughters of Bilitis, which operates on behalf of the lesbian.

These groups must be sharply distinguished from any informal homosexual rings that may exist primarily to promote sexual contacts and their publications (such as *Mattachine Review* and *One*) are serious efforts to bring together facts, commentaries, personal opinions, and literature on the topic—they have no connection with the male pin-up magazines (containing photographs or drawings of lightly clad musclemen) aimed mainly at a homosexual market. Meetings of these organizations—which often feature lectures by distinguished nonhomosexual experts or panel discussions of homosexual problems—may, of course, serve as a decorous occasion for meeting other individuals of like inclination. But the aim is clearly not proselytism. In fact Mattachine members are quoted by one reporter as saying:

> "On the basis of our own experience—the embarrassment, shame, and humiliation so many of us have known—we would definitely advise anybody who has not yet become an active homosexual, but has only misgivings about himself, to go the other way if he can." [63]

Whatever their public influence, these groups appear to function for some homosexuals as a symbol of hope and reassurance of the worthiness of their cause, and to provide some solace to those isolated homosexuals who may have felt left out of homosexual life as well as heterosexual society. For a few individuals, the organizations provide jobs, become their dominant interest, and absorb the bulk of their energies. There are a few "professional homosexuals"; protest movements within any category of the stigmatized may lead to "professionalization." [64]

Thus far the organizations, at least in this country, have extremely small memberships. According to one knowledgeable estimate, no more than 1 or 2 per cent of all homosexuals in the United States are even aware that these organizations exist.[65] Furthermore, fear of detection, apathy, and lack of conviction about the cause have all been cited as reasons for the relatively low level of support. Similarly, although there has been talk of developing a homosexual voting bloc, little has come of this political aspect of the movement. On the other hand, the gradually increasing freedom with which the organizations distribute their publications and otherwise communicate their views is cited as evidence of the movement's progress. In general, though, the evidence to date seems to support the comment that "homosexuals, *as a group,* aren't going to lead any revolt because the last thing they want is to get involved in any real struggle. They just want to be let alone. . . ." [66]

Identity Problems

Both in the process by which an individual recognizes himself to be a homosexual and in the reactions he has to such a realization, the responses of significant others must be crucially implicated. As Kitsuse has stated: "The critical feature of the deviant-defining process is not the behavior of individuals who are defined as deviant, but rather the interpretations others make of their behaviors, whatever those behaviors may be." [67] Although actual encounters with law enforcement agencies and other punitive experiences often establish or strongly reinforce a deviant self-image, more subtle processes may produce the same result. An exclusive homosexual orientation in adulthood must be viewed as an outcome of the individual's entire interpersonal development and reflects the initial expectations of others, the behavior he has exhibited, and the reactions of others to such behavior. Official definition as homosexual will, of course, strengthen the likelihood of a deviant outcome. Evelyn Hooker reports that she has encountered in her research many cases in which it appears that confirmed homosexuality was partly attributable to the individual's having—at one point—been labeled as homosexual (and even advised to accept the label) by some official agency.[68] There are also reports of individuals who did not realize they were basically homosexual until late in life. But, whenever the realization occurs and however gradually it develops, it must ordinarily be a disturbing one.

As Goffman has emphasized, the stigmatized individual shares many of the beliefs and understandings regarding identity that prevail in his society. His general conditioning in the culture alerts him to his own failure to meet the dominant criteria for social approval, and may even cause him to feel shame because of this shortcoming.[69] The "failing" of the homosexual must indeed be quite clear to him. Sex is one of the several "master status-determining traits." [70] Sexual orientation goes to the very heart of social and personal identity. It must be evident to the confirmed homosexual not only that his sexual inclinations disgust the "normals," but also that he is unable—or, at least, unwilling—to meet socially prescribed masculine-role expectations. Although some studies do reveal individual cases of "good adjustment," it is most unlikely that many confirmed homosexuals can view this state of affairs with complete equanimity.

There may be some individuals who can sporadically engage in homosexual behavior without finding the possibility of homosexual imputation seriously threatening. This appears to be true of the "beats" described by Polsky, who "accept homosexual experiences almost as casually as heterosexual ones." These individuals neither define themselves as homosexuals nor give up heterosexual activity. "Beats not only tolerate deviant sex roles but, to a much greater extent than previous bohemians, display a very high tolerance of sex-role ambiguity." [71] Very likely this casual bisexual orientation is possible in part because of the general social and political disaffiliation of these people. When one is almost totally alienated from prevailing values, when one hardly cares at all what people think (i.e., what "respectables" think) about one's behavior generally, society's disapproval of certain sexual behavior need not be a matter for concern. But this would seem to be a rather atypical outlook. Most confirmed homosexuals must find themselves confronted with a highly disturbing life situation. The ability to cope with it will depend not merely on the deviant's inner resources, but also on the extent to which he can obtain support from his fellow stigmatized and from significant others, avoid traumatically humiliating experiences, and still achieve satisfaction of his basic desires.

Group support cannot, however, entirely neutralize the factors working to undermine the homosexual's self-acceptance. To begin with, as just noted, the homosexual must experience confusion regarding his general identity as a male. The situation might be eased if homosexuals were simply men who would have preferred to have been women. This is not at all clear, however, from their behavior or their attitudes. Sometimes efforts are made to distinguish between the "passive" and the "active" homosexual—and some psychiatrists assert that the former really feels himself to be a woman, whereas the latter's disturbance is limited to inappropriate choice of a sexual object. Other observers feel that such a distinction is highly questionable. There is evidence that many homosexuals alternate between active and passive roles, and that there is no perfect correlation between masculinity or effeminacy and the assumption of one role or the other. According to Cory and LeRoy, most inverts "identify with and think of themselves as males at least as much as do their heterosexual counterparts. . . ." It is their recognition that society judges them to be not "real" men that fills them with insecurity, and that leads some homosexuals to a compulsive masculinity.[72] The behavior of, and the reaction of many homosexuals to, the "drag queen" or "swishy" invert illustrates further the confusions relating to sexual identity. It has been noted that the "queen," who looks, walks, and talks not like a woman but like a man masquerading as a woman, seeks to arouse "as much derision, indignation, condemnation, and official chagrin as possible without actually getting arrested as a public nuisance." [73] Conceivably, such flaunting behavior might represent spirited defiance. An equally likely interpretation, however, would emphasize a need for self-degradation and a wish for punishment. This type of homosexual is looked down on and often considered "sick" by many in the homosexual community as well as by heterosexuals.

Even when homosexuals are drawn neither to compulsive masculinity nor to extreme effeminacy, self-acceptance is still continually threatened both by contacts with "normals" and by certain aspects of homosexual life. The need for concealment becomes a key fact of existence, if not a constant preoccupation. As one invert has put it:

> I was forced to be deceitful, living one life during my working hours and another when I was free. I had two sets of friends; almost, one might say, two faces. At the back of my mind there was always a nagging fear that my two worlds might suddenly collide. . . .[74]

Goffman has properly suggested that passing need not always be accompanied by great anxiety.[75] Yet in the case of a homosexual with any considerable position in the community the anxieties will be very real, and there is evidence that such feelings are prevalent. The fact that the discreditable secret is a "criminal" one, and that its revelation might have significant legal consequences, increases the anxiety. (It is interesting that the term *straight* is used by homosexuals to describe the nonhomosexual way of life—just as it is used by professional criminals to describe the law-abiding way of life.) In some instances, anxiety over exposure and legal action may have dire consequences indeed:

> One recent case, that of a seventeen-year-old boy awaiting trial on a homosexual charge who hanged himself in his cell, prompted the judge to observe: "In a decent world an adolescent would not be prosecuted on a criminal charge arising out of a sexual offence. He would be handed over to some intelligent, sympathetic person who would help him out of his difficulties." In a research study of a group of suicides and attempted suicides selected at random, a homosexual element was discovered in half of them.[76]

Without doubt, such reactions are extreme, but at the very least the need almost continually to play a role, "to be on," [77] in any mixed settings must place a severe strain on the individual homosexual. Exacerbating this strain is the danger of inadvertent exposure to a law enforcement officer. The entrapment technique means that the homosexual must often interact within what has been called a "vulnerable frame." [78] Thus even when he is not passing for normal, the homosexual can never know when he may undergo the interpersonal humiliation as well as suffer the adverse practical consequences of discovering suddenly that the interaction he's engaged in is not really what it seemed to be.

In addition to problems posed by the possibilities of exposure, the homosexual is continually aware of the heterosexual's extreme contempt for his condition. Not only must the homosexual encounter this contempt, but usually there is little he can do about it. Describing a situation in which he felt compelled to smile at a "queer joke," Cory states: "I had debased my character by giving tacit consent and even approval to the abuse of which I felt I was personally the victim." [79] Although there may be some individuals so well adjusted to their deviance that they can take such incidents in their stride, more often Cory's conclusion would seem to hold true:

A person cannot live in an atmosphere of universal rejection, of widespread pretense, of a society that outlaws and banishes his activities and desires, of a social world that jokes and sneers at every turn, without a fundamental influence on his personality.[80]

That the homosexual is in fact disturbed by such contempt is suggested by the need he may feel to retaliate. The technique of rendering uncomfortable the "straight" visitor to a homosexual bar has already been mentioned. Rechy provides a fictional example— a Mardi Gras incident in which an unsuspecting male is led to kiss a homosexual in "drag" (i.e., dressed as a female), who then reveals his true gender.[81]

Certainly there is no simple or universally applicable description of the dominant feelings of homosexuals about their homosexuality. In her perceptive analysis of guilt and shame, Helen Merrell Lynd has noted that usually the former concept is applied to feelings about a specific act in violation of a social code; the latter concept relates more centrally to a generalized sense of deep personal inadequacy, of failure to live up to an ideal.[82] Negative self-conceptions arising from homosexuality would seem to fall in between, or in both, these categories. Homosexual behavior does involve specifically proscribed acts, yet ordinarily the "offense" is not discrete but rather a continuing one. At the same time, as suggested above, the condition of homosexuality is likely to give rise to general identity difficulties and considerable feelings of inadequacy. Whether one says that many homosexuals experience shame or guilt or both, at least it seems valid to assert that many suffer from some form of low self-esteem. Such poor self-acceptance relates partly to the very central matter of sexual identity, as such, and partly to the social condemnation and humiliation which invariably confronts homosexuals. It is also reinforced by the very patterns of sexual behavior to which homosexuals are driven by the need for concealment. One-night stands and commercial sex transactions have been said both to reflect and to increase the considerable ambivalence of the homosexual about his condition and his behavior.

In a very general sense the psychological impact on the homosexual is not unlike that experienced by the oppressed Negro:

> . . . his self-esteem suffers . . . because he is constantly receiving an unpleasant image of himself from the behavior of others to him. This is the subjective impact of social discrimination. . . . It seems to be an ever-present and unrelieved irritant.[83]

"Adjusted" Homosexuals

Findings in the Hooker studies (*see* p. 74) suggest that some homosexuals may be relatively well-adjusted individuals. The same researcher reports that many of her homosexual subjects displayed no indications of severe guilt. There does seem to be evidence here that, given relatively favorable conditions, some homosexuals may avoid serious psychological disturbance. Such findings are corroborated by the knowledge that many homosexuals are, in fact, functioning reasonably well (except, by prevailing standards, sexually) in modern society. Neither the self-destructive reaction nor the extremely antisocial reaction (where the homosexual breaks with all dominant norms) seems to represent a major adaptation. But this does not mean that identity ambivalence and low self-esteem may not still be present in many or even most cases. It is interesting that homosexual life is called "gay," but it would seem a mistake to infer from this that the invert society is a predominantly happy one. Homosexuals may feel genuine relief and some considerable pleasure in being able to drop the mask and meet with fellow inverts. Yet many observers have noted a forced gaiety in such activities, and in any case it is questionable whether the pleasurable aspects of the invert's life can often outweigh the frequent loneliness and insecurity. An informal survey among 100 male homosexuals found that while 75 per cent considered themselves generally well-adjusted, 57 per cent did admit to some adjustment difficulties, and 90 per cent reported some concern about exposure. In another study of 300 male inverts, all but a handful stated they did not want to change their own sexual orientation, but the same respondents overwhelmingly stated that they would not want their sons to be homosexuals.[84]

It has been suggested that a deviant is "adjusted" to the extent that there is a convergence between society's view of him and his view of himself.[85] From this perspective one can see the difficulty the homosexual has in adjusting to his deviance. Acceptance of the fact that he is homosexual would be an important first step, and apparently many inverts are able to take this step without extreme difficulty. It is unlikely, however, that many homosexuals can easily accept society's definition of them as inadequate males, nor can they gracefully slip into the circumscribed and often stereotyped role society would allow them. The homosexual can neither fully accept nor completely disavow society's judgment of his sexual inclinations and activities. The deviant social organization developed by homosexuals does help the individual adjust to his situation, but this group support is considerably more limited than that provided for, say, the professional criminal. The professional thief can convince himself that everybody's crooked, that everyone is out to get something so he might as well get it first. And whereas he is an outsider in the law-abiding world, he is an insider in the community of thieves. He knows full well, however, that in many important respects he is much like the people of the upperworld. The homosexual, on the other hand, is not merely an outsider in respectable society; he is labeled "sick" and "disgusting" as well as "immoral." He can engage in a protective fellowship with other inverts, but many of his fellow stigmatized are themselves not at all sure they are not "sick." Given this situation, it would seem likely that the fully adjusted homosexual is a rarity. The activities of the homophile movement, in developing an ideology supportive of homosexual behavior, may help some homosexuals to grapple with their problems; for many others an extremely uneasy self-acceptance is likely to persist.

Prevention and Treatment

Conceivably one could argue that no special public policy toward homosexuality is needed at all; an individual's sexual inclinations and behavior are strictly his own business, and inversion is just one of the possible alternatives from which people can choose. This view, according to which any attempt at controlling homosexuality is uncalled for, will be acceptable to few people in our society. There is a strong and sound belief that heterosexuality is the preferable adaptation (both for society and for the individual) and that homosexuality should at least be discouraged—to the extent that discouragement is possible. Furthermore, notwithstanding differences of opinion about the degree of psychopathology involved, there is good reason to think that full inversion is not simply an alternative that some people have freely chosen.

It is not at all clear, however, just what can be done to discourage or to prevent homosexuality. Although the causes are somewhat obscure, it seems likely that major alterations of social structure and culture would be necessary in order to reduce homosexuality to any significant degree. And if it is true that inversion is on the increase, then probably the stemming or even the reversal of broad social trends would also be required. A sharpening of sex-role differentiation, and an accompanying relaxation of the multiple burdens of the male role, might be seen as helping to curb any flight from masculinity. Yet, even assuming that this would be effective and that it could somehow be encouraged by policy, the strong current of social change in the opposite direction (i.e., toward "equalizing" the roles of men and women) would be a major obstacle. Prevention in individual cases may be a more realistic goal. The sympathetic counselling of young persons who seem to be heading in the direction of homosexuality may sometimes inhibit that adaptation. If such persons are reached early enough, the likelihood of success would be increased.

Along with preventive measures one can expect therapists to undertake treatment efforts in cases of confirmed adult homosexuality. Discussions of treatment have sometimes become misdirected owing to the belief that homosexuality might be completely or largely eliminated. This appears to be a highly unrealistic hope, and indeed there is some reason to think that overconcentration on cure (in the sense of complete sexual reorientation) has often hampered treatment attempts. Hormone therapy has not proven of significant value in altering homosexual desires or behavior. According to one report, aversion therapy (in which the patient is conditioned to react negatively to homosexual stimuli and positively to heterosexual ones) may hold out some possibilities.[86]

A PROMISING REPORT

Most psychotherapists remain pessimistic about the likelihood of effecting complete reversals of sex orientation. One recent treatment-research program, however, has provided some basis for greater optimism. Of the 106 homosexual cases treated psychoanalytically by Bieber and his co-workers, twenty-nine patients (27 per cent) became exclusively heterosexual during the course of treatment. Though this is a higher success figure than has usually been reported, it is still noteworthy that in 73 per cent of the cases the treatment was unsuccessful. It is also significant that the initial status of fifteen of the twenty-nine "cured" patients was reported as "bisexual," that a much higher proportion of those who were cured than of those who were not had expressed the wish to overcome homosexuality, and that the duration of treatment was a crucial factor influencing the outcome (eighteen of the twenty-nine successes involved 350 or more therapy hours each). A history that included attempts at heterosexual intercourse prior to entering therapy was also found to be prognostically favorable. Another noteworthy finding—one which would stand despite these limitations on the "cure" data—was that in 97 of the homosexual patients, therapy did produce general improvement not directly related to sexual problems.[87]

Even assuming that the Bieber patients represented a reasonable sampling of homosexuals (an assumption for which there is little or no basis), it seems clear that any "cure" requires lengthy and ordinarily very costly treatment, that it depends crucially on adequate motivation and probably on certain aspects of past history, and that in any case the probability of full success remains small. But even the initiation of such a process is unlikely for the vast majority of inverts, many of whom appear to be uninterested in changing. Though few may be fully convinced that they are as normal as anybody else, many definitely resist the claim that they are demonstrably suffering from a psychic disorder. And as some of the Bieber case histories show, there are adult homosexuals who have never attempted heterosexual intercourse, do not report heterosexual dream content, and in general do not even find women very attractive sexually. There is every reason to believe that Cory and LeRoy are correct in asserting that "the vast majority of homosexuals cannot or will not see a therapist for any effective length of time in the course of their lifetime." The same writers suggest further that, for those individuals who have integrated homosexuality into their general pattern of living, psychiatric interference may actually be harmful—in that it may remove their only basis for a fairly stable personal identity.[88]

Under such circumstances, it seems evident that the impact of voluntary treatment must be limited, and that the efficacy of compulsory treatment—assuming it were possible to locate and forcibly to treat a large proportion of existing inverts—would be practically nil. Both preventive measures and voluntary therapy, aimed primarily at increasing the patient's over-all adjustment and only secondarily at reorienting him sexually, deserve continuation. Neither, however, can be expected to provide any ultimate solution of the problem, or to lead to its total or even substantial elimination.

The Law

What are the prospects for controlling homosexuality through the criminal law? Under present laws and law enforcement measures, only a slight incursion is made into homosexual life. It is difficult to see how a policy of more stringent penalties and stepped-up enforcement would improve the situation. Presumably the chief aim of such a policy would be deterrence, and although harsh sanctions might effectively deter some individuals who now engage sporadically and noncompulsively in homosexual acts, it is most unlikely to affect those who have an exclusive homosexual orientation. But, above all, the low visibility of homosexual behavior and the mixed public reaction to the punishment of homosexuals would make such a policy unworkable. As it is, the police are not fully enforcing existing provisions and the courts are not imposing maximum penalties. And almost everyone agrees that imprisonment is no sensible treatment for the homosexual; in fact, a well-known criticism of the prison system is that it breeds homosexual behavior. *Permanent* isolation of untreatable homosexual offenders might partly prevent the "contamination" of the public, yet—apart from humanistic and civil libertarian objections to such a step—there would simply be no practicable means of putting it into effect.

One is left with the conclusion that neither present policy nor a stiffer enforcement of that policy can significantly curb homosexual behavior. The fact that present laws may contribute to certain secondary features of the problem gives importance to the Wolfenden report and similar proposals for partial legalization of homosexuality. It should be emphasized that these recommendations are of a limited nature: only homosexual acts between consenting adults in private would be placed outside the legal proscriptions. Male prostitution, the use of force, the involvement of minors, and public displays would still be subject to punishment. Furthermore, it would be a mistake to consider such proposals highly radical; on the contrary, such an exception is written into the criminal law of most continental European countries, and as one survey has pointed out:

"Abolition by no means implies indifference to the phenomenon and the problems of homosexuality." [89]

RESISTANCE TO LEGAL CHANGE

There are many reasons why there is strong resistance to the adoption of such reform proposals. It is often argued that homosexuality is both unnatural and immoral. It has been shown that there may be some anthropological basis for believing that the capacity for homosexual behavior is, in fact, quite natural. On the other hand, many would assert that the actual tendency toward such behavior is, at least, less natural than that toward heterosexual behavior. But in any case "unnaturalness," alone, would not seem to be an adequate basis for legal proscription. Nor is immorality a satisfactory ground for legal proscription. Actually even theologians disagree as to the invariable immorality (or at least the moral culpability) of inversion. Sherwin Bailey, in his careful analysis of the theological and moral aspects of homosexuality, concluded that, although all homosexual acts are themselves "intrinsically sinful," there are instances (usually involving the genuine invert) in which "homosexual acts must be considered as committed in a state of invincible ignorance [*ignorance* refers here to lack of full and proper understanding of the moral import of the conduct], and for these the agent cannot morally be blamed. . . ." [90]

But the overriding objection to the "immorality" argument concerns the effort to make the criminal law coextensive with the realm of morals. The Wolfenden Committee asserted that it was "not charged to enter into matters of private moral conduct except in so far as they directly affect the public good. . . ." It saw the function of the criminal law in the field of sexual behavior as being "to preserve public order and decency, to protect the citizen from what is offensive or injurious, and to provide sufficient safeguards against exploitation and corruption of others, particularly those who are specially vulnerable. . . ." It went on to assert: "It is not, in our view, the function of the law to intervene in the private lives of citizens, or to seek to enforce any particular pattern of behavior, further than is necessary to carry out the purposes we have outlined." [91] It is significant that in statements presented to the Com-

mittee, both the Church of England Moral Welfare Council and a
British Roman Catholic advisory committee had subscribed to this
distinction between immorality and crime—as have numerous individual theologians in both Britain and America. At least one eminent jurist, Lord Devlin, has argued against this line of reasoning,
asserting that "the suppression of vice is as much the law's business
as the suppression of subversive activities," and that sometimes a
function of the criminal law is "to enforce a moral principle and
nothing else." H. L. A. Hart, a leading legal philosopher, has in
turn been highly critical of Devlin's reasoning. As Hart has emphasized, "there is very little evidence to support the idea that morality
is best taught by fear of legal punishment," nor is there any reason
to feel that "the mere expression of moral condemnation [is] a thing
of value in itself," to be pursued at any cost.[92]

It is sometimes maintained that public opinion would not accept
more permissive legislation, and indeed this was the declared basis
for the British government's decision not to implement the Wolfenden recommendations. Actually, knowledge of public attitudes
toward homosexuality is extremely meager. The Wolfenden Committee stated that it relied on "our estimate of the standards of the
community in general," but provided no indication as to how such
an estimate was made. Likewise, it has been noted that in the fram-
ing of the American Law Institute's recommendation on this issue,
the crucial determination was reached through council vote (35 to
24)—with proponents of opposing views differing sharply as to their
estimates of the community's moral evaluation of the behavior in
question.[93] Further research clearly would be helpful to policy formulation in this area. Opponents of reform frequently assume public punitiveness toward homosexuality, but some research findings
suggest that public attitudes are not at all clear-cut. Thus Kitsuse,
reporting on a study involving more than 700 subjects, notes that,
"while reactions toward persons defined as homosexuals tend to be
negatively toned, they are far from homogeneous as to the forms or
intensity of the sanctions invoked and applied," and concludes: "In
view of the extreme negative sanctions against homosexuality which
are posited on theoretical grounds, the generally mild reactions of
our subjects are striking." [94] In a small-scale study undertaken by
this writer, only 16 per cent of the student respondents chose reac-

tions considered punitive ("should be punished, but not severely"
or "should be severely punished"), when asked to evaluate the cir
cumstance: "Two unmarried adults engaging, by mutual consen
and in private, in homosexual acts." [95]

Even if it be assumed that the dominant public opinion in ou
society strongly opposes any liberalization of homosexuality laws, i
must be recognized that such opinion is not merely the basis for
but also partly a reflection of, existing policy. Furthermore, som
analysts would suggest that legislation on such matters should oc
casionally be used in an effort to spur changes in public attitude:

> It is not and should not be a principle of government that social
> reform must wait upon a favorable plebiscite. No plebiscite dictated
> the reform of the Factory Acts in the 1870's. It is possible even that,
> had a vote been taken, a majority would have been found against
> reform: for many people believed that it was wrong and futile for
> the state to interfere in such economic questions, and many of the
> factory workers themselves were against the abolition of child labor,
> because they did not see how they could survive without the money
> that their children earned.[96]

In any case, the gradual breakdown of the conspiracy of silence
which often surrounds such topics as homosexuality will both pro
vide greater access to existing public attitudes and effect certain
changes in such attitudes. As the chairman of the Wolfenden Com
mittee has written: "I believe that the fact of our having reported,
and reported in the sense in which we did, has helped to create a
more informed public opinion than existed before." [97]

CONSEQUENCES OF LAW REFORM

Some observers seem to feel that the relaxation of laws on ho
mosexuality might seriously threaten the central role of the family
in society. It is quite true that control over homosexuality serves to
strengthen the position of the family and to reinforce sex-role dif
ferentiation.[98] But this fact hardly provides a basis for wholesale
legal and social persecution of inverts. Surely it is fantastic to think
that enactment of the proposed reform would impel hordes of in
dividuals immediately to discard their current heterosexual incli

nations and activities for a life of homosexuality, thus precipitating the decline and eventual demise of the conventional family and of civilization as we know it. Apart from the erroneous assumption that the homosexual impulse is the more compelling or attractive, this reasoning is quite out of line with the evidence from the many countries which have held private adult homosexuality to be a matter with which the law should not attempt to deal. The situation is complicated, too, by the fact that a good many homosexuals do actually marry and even have children—notwithstanding their predominantly inverted inclinations and their occasional or frequent part-time involvement in the homosexual life. Similarly, concern about the recruitment of minors by the so-called predatory homosexual,[99] is probably exaggerated. As has been shown, there is a likelihood that the causal significance of seduction may be overemphasized. Anyway, it is not clear why elimination of the legal ban on the private acts of consenting adults should increase the dangers of seduction. Since acts with like-minded adults would become somewhat freer, acts with minors might be expected to decrease.

Of course there is no authoritative basis for a prediction of the specific long-range consequences of legal revision in this area. In his statement of reservations to the Wolfenden Report, one Committee member, James Adair, expressed grave concern regarding the element of condonation possibly implied by relaxation of the homosexuality laws. Adair also suggested that those proposing elimination of a long-standing criminal law provision must sustain the burden of proof regarding justification of such a change.[100] The majority of the Committee, on the other hand, appeared to accept the contrary notion—that the burden of proof lies, rather, with those seeking to control behavior by means of the criminal law. It must be admitted that the proposed reform would seem to imply less disapproval of homosexual practices than is currently institutionalized through law. At the same time, it must be stressed that less disapproval is not the same thing as positive approval. And the argument, made by Lord Hailsham in the British debates,[101] that retention of the repressive law might be justified precisely because it is not rigorously enforced, will strike many as both hypocritical and inadvisable from the standpoint of maintaining a sound legal order.

One can argue that, given the highly incomplete nature of present knowledge, any new legislation should await further research:

> Although the history of legal control of sex conduct is largely one of failure, this fact is a commentary on the problem of enforceability of the law; it does not, of itself, establish anything about the degree of social danger of the conduct. It is always possible to argue . . . that conditions could be worse were the laws not on the books.[102]

On the other hand, the failure of current policy lies not merely in unenforceability (i.e., its failure to curb homosexuality). Repression does more—it reinforces some of the social dangers involved, and very likely creates others. Furthermore, it is highly unlikely, no matter how much research is undertaken, that there will ever be any real semblance of empirical proof regarding long-term consequences. At the same time, because policy is ongoing, policymakers cannot in good faith insist that they are waiting for the fruits of further research; if they resist change, they must at least recognize that they prefer to go along with present policies rather than to take a chance on new ones. Short-run comparative evidence from the countries that have adopted more permissive legislation suggests that, under such laws, overt antisocial behavior is unlikely to increase. It would seem that the policy decisions depend upon the placement of burden of proof. Advocates of reform cannot demonstrate uncontrovertibly the over-all benefits of change; yet those who support retention of the present laws have been far from effective in justifying public interference with private conduct in this area.

The discussion of policy has thus far focused largely on "rational" arguments pro and con. But it is important to recognize also that present policies may serve significant latent functions for society and for particular individuals. As just noted, such policies may indirectly help to strengthen the family as a social institution. Also, the present institutionalized reactions to homosexuality establish a segregative pattern that proves functional for the dominant yet somewhat ambivalent majority. This structural ambivalence, if it may be called that, undoubtedly has roots in individual outlooks. It has frequently been noted that the punishment of any "criminal" or deviant is an opportunity for the socially sanctioned release of hostility and aggression among the "law-abiding" citizens, as well as for a relief from guilt concerning their own deviant impulses. It has also been suggested by various writers that Americans seem unusually preoccupied with, or concerned about, homosexuality. And many psychiatrists assert that those who speak out most loudly for harsh treatment of the homosexual often do so because they themselves are plagued by doubts and fears suggestive of latent homosexuality. If this is so, the invert may provide not merely a convenient scapegoat for free-floating aggression, but also for some individuals a significant vehicle for vicarious punishment: "By punishing him we are not only showing him that he can't 'get away with it' but holding him up as a terrifying example to our own tempted and rebellious selves." [103]

Summary

The present discussion has included relatively little consideration of possible causes of homosexuality. This is intentional. Research into the causes of homosexuality should continue, as should whatever preventive and therapeutic measures can be taken in individual cases, but not in the expectation that any startling breakthrough will provide a widely applicable "cure" or a general "solution" for this social problem. The position taken here is that it is more useful to focus on the question of public policy in this area and to seek control over any secondary aspects of the problem that specific policies may breed.

Even if the exact nature and extent of its influence are not known, there is little doubt that society's reaction (both informal and formal) significantly shapes the problem of homosexuality. The causes of inversion—i.e., confirmed homosexuality, as contrasted with homosexual acts resorted to in sex-segregated situations or performed occasionally in quest of variety—are somewhat obscure, but a key feature is the process by which others identify and deal with the individual in question as a homosexual and through which he eventually comes to view himself as one. Whatever identity problems the invert may have as a result of his sexual condition are exacerbated by his being labeled a criminal, and being forced to conceal his condition if he wishes to participate in respectable social activities. The homosexual subculture provides some collective support and comraderie, but even the organized homosexual life exhibits characteristics that may undermine the invert's self-acceptance and morale.

Laws against homosexual acts do not significantly control the proscribed behavior. The extremely low visibility under which the acts may occur, the lack of a complainant, and the ambiguous nature of public support combine to make these laws highly unenforceable. Given the peculiar supply-demand situation, repressive law does not in this instance (as it does in the case of abortion) primarily breed a large and profitable illicit traffic supplying the demanded service (unless the development of male prostitution may be partly attributed to this repression). The most evident results of antihomosexuality laws are the heightening of the invert's vulnerability to blackmail and other forms of exploitation, and the encouragement of police corruption and repressive enforcement procedures. Secondary results consist of the impact on the homosexual himself—his attitude toward his sexual inclinations, his view of society generally, and of course the specific types of practical discrimination he experiences and the demoralizing and humiliating behavior into which he is pushed.

These laws, in short, make a good many individuals more unhappy than they would otherwise be, without showing any short-run signs of effectively dealing with the problem of homosexuality. They help to create an aggrieved minority, and nurture the kind of public reaction that unwittingly promotes the more disapproved types of homosexual behavior. The long-run consequences of a less repressive policy are not absolutely clear, but there is no evidence that such a policy need result in either a substantial increase in homosexuality or in any of the associated problems. Recent years have seen a distinct trend toward a more humane and sensible attitude toward the invert, and this has involved not only specific proposals for legal reform but also a more general breakdown of the conspiracy of silence that has traditionally surrounded the topic.

Notes

[1] Committee on Homosexual Offences and Prostitution, *Report*, Cmnd. 247 (London: Her Majesty's Stationery Office, 1957); published in the United States as *The Wolfenden Report* (New York: Stein and Day, 1963). See also Edwin Schur, "The Wolfenden Report," *American Sociological Review*, 28 (December 1963), 1055.

[2] Hendrik M. Ruitenbeek (ed.), *The Problem of Homosexuality in Modern Society* (New York: E. P. Dutton & Co., Inc., 1963), pp. xi, xiv.

[3] Robert Lindner, "Homosexuality and the Contemporary Scene," in *Must You Conform?* (New York: Grove Press, 1961), pp. 31-76.

[4] William J. Helmer, "New York's 'Middle-Class' Homosexuals," *Harpers* (March 1963), 87. This observation, which refers to the "better class of 'gay' bar," may well be a highly selective one. However it does illustrate the general point that the popular stereotype in many instances does not hold true.

[5] Lindner, *op. cit.*, pp. 36, 37.

[6] Derrick Sherwin Bailey (ed.), *Sexual Offenders and Social Punishment* (London: Church of England Moral Welfare Council, 1956), p. 26. The Council further commented that "the whole problem of inversion has been obscured and narrowed by too exclusive a concern with sexual acts . . ." (p. 28).

[7] Erving Goffman, *Stigma: Notes on the Management of Spoiled Identity* (Englewood Cliffs, N.J.: Prentice-Hall, Inc., 1963), pp. 143-44.

[8] Irving Bieber, *et al.*, *Homosexuality: A Psychoanalytic Study* (New York: Basic Books, Inc., 1962), p. 306.

[9] *Ibid.*, p. 173.

[10] See Abram Kardiner, "The Flight from Masculinity," and other selections in Ruitenbeek, *op. cit.*

[11] *American Journal of Psychiatry*, 107 (April 1951), 786, as reprinted in Bieber, *et al.*, *op. cit.*, p. 275.

[12] Clellan Ford and Frank Beach, *Patterns of Sexual Behavior* (New York; Ace Books, 1951), p. 150.

[13] Bieber, *et al.*, *op. cit.*, p. 305.

[14] Lindner, *op. cit.*, pp. 40-41.

[15] Simone de Beauvoir, *The Second Sex*, translated by Parshley (New York: Alfred A. Knopf, Inc., 1952), p. 424.

[16] Albert Ellis, *The American Sexual Tragedy* (New York: Grove Press, 1962), p. 94.

[17] Evelyn Hooker, "The Adjustment of the Male Overt Homosexual," in Ruitenbeek *op. cit.*

[18] John Kitsuse, "Societal Reaction to Deviant Behavior: Problems of Theory and Method," *Social Problems*, 9 (Winter 1962), 247-56.

[19] Bieber, *et al.*, *op. cit.*, p. 192.

[20] Alfred C. Kinsey, W. B. Pomeroy, and C. E. Martin, *Sexual Behavior in the Human Male* (Philadelphia: W. B. Saunders Co., 1948).

[21] Jess Stearn, *The Sixth Man* (New York: Macfadden Books, 1962).

[22] Kardiner, *op. cit.*

[23] Committee on Homosexual Offences and Prostitution, *op. cit.*, p. 20.

[24] Frank S. Caprio, *Female Homosexuality* (New York: Grove Press, 1962), p. 71.

[25] Donald W. Cory and John P. LeRoy, *The Homosexual and His Society: A View From Within* (New York: The Citadel Press, 1963), p. 160.

[26] This point was suggested by David Matza.

[27] The Connecticut statute is typical: "Bestiality and Sodomy. Any person who has carnal copulation with any beast, or who has carnal knowledge of any man, against the order of nature, unless forced or under fifteen years of age, shall be imprisoned in the State prison for not more than thirty years." Revised Statutes, 1958 revision. C. 944, sec. 53-216.

[28] Norman St. John-Stevas, *Life, Death and the Law* (Bloomington: Indiana University Press, 1961), p. 199. For a reasonably up-to-date presentation of the specific state laws relating to homosexuality, see Appendix X of that work.

[29] Morris Ploscowe, *Sex and the Law,* rev. ed. (New York: Ace Books, 1962), p. 188.

Variation and definitional vagueness leave somewhat obscure exactly what acts are prohibited under certain of the laws, but it is generally clear that anal intercourse (in some jurisdictions the meaning of *sodomy* is strictly limited to this act) and oral-genital relations—the sexual acts most frequently engaged in by homosexuals—are everywhere proscribed. Other behavior, such as mutual masturbation, or "indecent assaults," may be punishable under further provisions. Because few of these statutes stipulate partners of the same sex, actually they are not directed at homosexual behavior alone but cover some heterosexual behavior as well. Not only has this confused the very definition of the term *homosexual,* but it has also meant that at least theoretically heterosexual couples (even husbands and wives) might be punishable for behavior that is prevalent in heterosexual relations.

[30] Peter Wildeblood, *Against the Law* (London: Penguin Books, Inc., 1955), p. 61.

[31] C. H. Rolph, "The Problem for the Police," *New Statesman* (June 25, 1960), 945.

[32] *Kelly v. U.S.,* 194 F. 2d 150 (1951), as reprinted in R. C. Donnelly, J. Goldstein, and R. D. Schwartz, *Criminal Law* (New York: The Free Press of Glencoe, Inc., 1962), p. 180.

[33] See *Vallerga v. Dept. of Alcoholic Beverage Control* (1960), and other cases cited therein, *ibid.*, pp. 185-87.

[34] Cory and LeRoy, *op. cit.*, p. 107.

[35] Helmer, *op. cit.*, p. 86.

[36] Frederick W. Egen, *Plainclothesman: A Handbook of Vice and Gambling Investigation* (New York: Arco Publishing Co., Inc., 1952), pp. 8-9. Recently a Deputy Police Commissioner of New York City was reported to have acknowledged that enforcement efforts have been limited to suppression of public indecency and approaches to minors. "No attempt is made," he says, "to enforce the theoretical ban on private homosexual conduct between consenting adults." Robert C. Doty, "Growth of Overt Homosexuality Provokes Wide Concern," *The New York Times, Western Edition,* December 27, 1963, p. 7.

[37] As reprinted in J. T. Rees and H. V. Usill (eds.), *They Stand Apart* (New York: The Macmillan Company, 1955).

[38] Chic Conwell, *The Professional Thief: By a Professional Thief,* edited by Edwin H. Sutherland (Chicago: Phoenix Books, 1937, 1956), pp. 79-80. See also Ploscowe, *op. cit.,* pp. 195-96.

[39] Donald W. Cory, *The Homosexual in America: A Subjective Approach,* 2nd ed. (New York: Castle Books, 1960), p. 55.

[40] For the subcommittee's report, and for documents on veterans' benefits, see *ibid.,* Appendix A, pp. 269-80.

[41] Goffman, *op. cit.,* Chap. 2.

[42] Sherri Cavan, "Interaction in Home Territories," *Berkeley Journal of Sociology,* 8 (1963), 27.

[43] Albert K. Cohen, *Delinquent Boys: The Culture of the Gang.* (New York: The Free Press of Glencoe, Inc., 1955), p. 59.

[44] I am grateful to H. Laurence Ross for developing this point in discussion with me.

[45] Goffman, *op. cit.,* p. 81.

[46] See Cavan, *op. cit.,* especially pp. 28-31.

[47] Cory and LeRoy, *op. cit.,* pp. 122,123.

[48] Helmer, *op. cit.,* p. 87.

[49] Cory and LeRoy, *op. cit.,* p. 20.

[50] Maurice Leznoff and William A. Westley, "The Homosexual Community," *Social Problems,* 3 (April 1956), 257-63.

[51] Cory and LeRoy, *op. cit.,* p. 96.

[52] Albert J. Reiss, Jr., "The Social Integration of Queers and Peers," *Social Problems,* 9 (Fall 1961), 102-20; and "Sex Offenses: The Marginal Status of the Adolescent," *Law and Contemporary Problems,* 25 (Spring 1960), 309-33. See also H. Laurence Ross, "The 'Hustler' in Chicago," *Journal of Student Research,* 1 (September 1959), 13-19; and Simon Raven, "Boys Will be Boys: The Male Prostitute in London," in Ruitenbeek, *op. cit.*

[53] Cory and LeRoy, *op. cit.,* pp. 99, 100.

[54] See John Rechy, *City of Night* (New York: Grove Press, 1963), p. 36.

[55] Helmer, *op. cit.,* p. 91.

[56] Ned Polsky, "The Village Beat Scene: Summer 1960," *Dissent,* 8 (Summer 1961), 342; see also James Baldwin, *Another Country* (New York: Dial Press, 1962).

[57] For an interesting discussion of different "levels" of homosexual life in England, see Gordon Westwood, *Society and the Homosexual* (New York: E. P. Dutton & Co., Inc., 1953).

[58] Leznoff and Westley, *op. cit.,* p. 260.

[59] Howard S. Becker, *Outsiders: Studies in the Sociology of Deviance* (New York: The Free Press of Glencoe, Inc., 1963), pp. 35-36.

[60] Goffman, *op. cit.,* p. 20.

[61] Cory, *op. cit.,* p. 47.

[62] See Lindner, *op. cit.,* p. 74.

[63] Stearn, *op. cit.,* p. 161.

[64] See Goffman, *op. cit.,* pp. 24-28.

[65] Cory and LeRoy, *op. cit.,* p. 247.

[66] David McReynolds, "The Gay Underground—A Reply to Mr. Krim," in

D. Wolf and E. Fancher (eds.), *The Village Voice Reader* (New York: Grove Press, 1963), p. 152. See also Seymour Krim, "Revolt of the Homosexual," *ibid.*, pp. 146-51.

[67] Kitsuse, *op. cit.*, p. 255.

[68] Evelyn Hooker, "Homosexuality," in E. and W. Genné (eds.) *Foundations for Christian Family Policy* (New York: National Council of Churches, 1961), p. 174.

[69] Goffman, *op. cit.*, p. 7.

[70] See Everett Hughes, "Dilemmas and Contradictions of Status," *American Journal of Sociology*, 50 (March 1945), 353-59.

[71] Polsky, *op. cit.*, p. 348.

[72] Cory and LeRoy, *op. cit.*, p. 82.

[73] *Ibid.*, p. 67.

[74] Wildeblood, *op. cit.*, p. 37.

[75] Goffman, *op. cit.*, p. 87.

[76] Kenneth Robinson, "The Time for Decision," *New Statesman* (June 25, 1960), 943.

[77] Sheldon L. Messinger, *et al.*, "Life as Theater: Some Notes on the Dramaturgic Approach to Social Reality," *Sociometry*, 25 (March 1962), 98-109; see also Erving Goffman, *The Presentation of Self in Everyday Life* (Garden City, N.Y.: Doubleday & Company, Inc., 1959).

[78] Erving Goffman, in a lecture delivered at the University of California at Berkeley, December 12, 1963.

[79] Cory, *op. cit.*, p. 11.

[80] *Ibid.*, p. 12.

[81] Rechy, *op. cit.*, pp. 368-69.

[82] Helen Merrell Lynd, *On Shame and the Search for Identity* (New York: Science Editions, 1958).

[83] Abram Kardiner and Lionel Ovesey, *The Mark of Oppression: Explorations in the Personality of the American Negro* (New York: Meridian Books, Inc., 1962), pp. 302-303.

[84] Referred to in Bieber, *et al.*, *op. cit.*, p. 38; and Cory and LeRoy, *op. cit.*, p. 237.

[85] Edwin Lemert, *Social Pathology* (New York: McGraw-Hill Book Company, Inc., 1951), p. 91.

[86] See David Perlman, "Study of Sex Offenders: Research Into a Vast Area of Ignorance," *San Francisco Chronicle*, December 11, 1963, p. 56.

[87] See Bieber, *et al.*, *op. cit.*, Chap. XI.

[88] Cory and LeRoy, *op. cit.*, pp. 236, 237.

[89] H. A. Hammelmann, "Homosexuality and the Law in Other Countries," in Rees and Usill, *op. cit.*, p. 180.

[90] Derrick Sherwin Bailey, "The Homosexual and Christian Morals," in Bailey, *op. cit.*, p. 81.

[91] Committee on Homosexual Offences and Prostitution, *op. cit.*, p. 81.

[92] For a full account of this controversy see H. L. A. Hart, *Law, Liberty and Morality* (Stanford: Stanford University Press, 1963); also J. E. Hall Williams, "Sex Offenses: The British Experience," *Law and Contemporary Problems*, 25 (Spring 1960), 334-60.

[93] See documents in Donnelly, *et al.*, *op cit.*, pp. 124-36.

[94] Kitsuse, *op. cit.*, pp. 255, 256.

[95] Merrill A. Needham and Edwin M. Schur, "Student Punitiveness Toward Sexual Deviation," *Marriage and Family Living*, 25 (May 1963), 227-28. See also Arnold Rose and E. E. Prell, "Does the Punishment Fit the Crime? A Study in Social Valuation," *American Journal of Sociology*, 61 (November 1955), 247-59; and G. M. Gilbert, "Crime and Punishment: An Exploratory Comparison of Public, Criminal and Penological Attitudes," *Mental Hygiene*, 42 (October 1958), 550-57.

[96] A. J. Ayer, "Homosexuals and the Law," *New Statesman* (June 25, 1960), 941.

[97] J. F. Wolfenden, "Ahead of Public Opinion?", *New Statesman* (June 25, 1960), 941.

[98] See Talcott Parsons and Robert F. Bales, *Family, Socialization and Interaction Process* (New York: The Free Press of Glencoe, Inc., 1955).

[99] Hervey Cleckley, *The Caricature of Love* (New York: The Ronald Press Company, 1957); see excerpt reprinted in William Petersen and David Matza (eds.), *Social Controversy* (Belmont, Calif.: Wadsworth Publishing Co., 1963), pp. 145-53.

[100] See Committee on Homosexual Offenses and Prostitution, *op. cit.*, pp. 117-23.

[101] Viscount Hailsham, "Homosexuality and Society," in Rees and Usill, *op. cit.*, p. 32.

[102] Stanton Wheeler, "Sex Offenses: A Sociological Critique," *Law and Contemporary Problems*, 25 (Spring 1960), 262.

[103] J. C. Flugel, *Man, Morals and Society: A Psychoanalytic Study* (New York: International Universities Press, 1945), p. 169; see also Charles Berg, *Fear, Punishment, Anxiety and the Wolfenden Report* (London: George Allen & Unwin, 1959).

DRUG ADDICTION

The "Dope Fiend" Myth

In recent years there has been considerable repudiation of the once prevalent "dope fiend" myth[1]—which depicted the drug addict as a degenerate and vicious criminal much given to violent crimes and sex orgies. More and more people are coming to understand the nature of opiate drugs and the meaning of addiction. This discussion will be concerned primarily with that class of pain-killing and soothing drugs derived from or equivalent to opium. Morphine and heroin are the best known of these drugs; others include codeine, meperidine (Demerol), and methadone (Amidone, Dolophine). Such pain-killers are the drugs of choice of most persons who are fully addicted in the sense described below. This is an important point, because the continued use of these opiate-type drugs (to which the term *narcotics* may also be applied) produces characteristics and behavior quite at odds with stereotyped conceptions of the dope addict.

EFFECTS OF OPIATES

Central to the various common misconceptions is the belief that the addict is dangerously "hopped up." Actually, opiates are depressants—that is, they produce a general lowering of the level of nervous and other bodily activity. The effects of these drugs have been summarized as follows:

The depressant actions include analgesia (relief of pain), sedation (freedom from anxiety, muscular relaxation, decreased motor activity), hypnosis (drowsiness and lethargy), and euphoria (a sense of well-being and contentment).[2]

Although the relation between addiction and criminality will be examined, there is nothing about the operation of these drugs which would incline a user to commit criminal offenses. In fact, the specific effects of opiates, serve to decrease the likelihood of any violent antisocial behavior. Similarly, opiates produce a marked diminishing of the sexual appetite—long-term addiction producing impotence among most male addicts; hence, concern about "dope fiend sex orgies" is quite unfounded. Indeed, perhaps the most striking characteristic of addicts is their general inactivity—on the basis of which they might be considered unproductive or withdrawn but hardly fearsome.[3]

It has also been widely believed that opiates produce definite and extreme organic disturbance and deterioration in the users. Yet, as an authoritative report recently emphasized, there are no known organic diseases associated with chronic opiate addiction—such as are produced by alcohol addiction, regular cigarette-smoking, and even chronic overeating. Although opiate use does produce such effects as pupillary constriction, constipation, and sexual impotence, none of these conditions need be fully disabling, nor are they permanent.[4] Similarly, many characteristics and ailments, such as unkempt appearance and symptoms of malnutrition, which often are exhibited by addicts in our society, are attributable to the difficulties they experience in obtaining drugs rather than to the drugs' direct effects.

There is also considerable misunderstanding about the supposedly positive feelings the addict receives from the drugs. As noted above, a sense of well-being and contentment is often produced by opiates. As a young female addict has put it:

You simply do not worry about things you worried about before. You look at them in a different way. . . . Everything is always cool, everything is all right. It makes you not feel like fighting the world. . . . I mean it's that sort of a thing, you know, when you're *not* hooked.[5]

Some discussions of addiction have exaggerated the positive nature of these euphoric effects, and this has led to the widespread belief that addicts take drugs solely for "kicks." The crucial misunderstanding is suggested by the addict's express limitation of the above description of euphoria to *when you're* not *hooked*. In most cases, positive feelings about the drug are largely restricted to the early stages of addiction. In the later stages, a reversal of effects occurs, in which the drug is no longer taken primarily to obtain positive pleasure but rather to avoid the negative effects of withdrawal.[6] As the addict just quoted goes on to say, the user's feeling about the drug changes drastically once real dependence upon it is reached: "Suddenly, the character of taking off [injecting the drug] changes . . . all you're trying to do is keep from getting ill, really. . . ." [7] Indeed, the theory of "kicks" may be inadequate even when applied to the early stages of addiction. As one major research report has noted, the "kicks" adolescent addicts seek may reflect their overwhelming general unhappiness. To the extent that the drug combats this unhappiness, it primarily offers relief rather than positive pleasure. The same report also refers to interesting laboratory findings of wide variation in individual responses to an initial injection of opiates. These data suggest that even if such drugs tend to produce some euphoria, the nature and extent of this feeling may be greatly affected by the user's personality characteristics.[8]

THE ADDICTION PROCESS

The process of becoming addicted involves a developing bondage to the drug. According to a World Health Organization definition:

> Drug addiction is a state of periodic or chronic intoxication produced by the repeated consumption of a drug (natural or synthetic). Its characteristics include: (1) an overpowering desire or need (compulsion) to continue taking the drug and to obtain it by any means; (2) a tendency to increase the dose; (3) a psychic (psychological) and generally a physical dependence on the effects of the drug; (4) an effect detrimental to the individual and to society.[9]

The term *intoxication* may not be the most appropriate to use in describing the effects of opiates, and there is at least some dispute about the nature and extent of detriment necessarily associated with addiction. However, the rest of the definition does highlight the crucial features of the addiction process. Tolerance and dependence are the characteristics which distinguish the confirmed addict from other drug users. *Tolerance* refers to the process through which the body adapts to the effects of a drug. Because of such adaptation, the dose must increase in size if the same effects are to be produced; likewise, with the growth of tolerance the drug user becomes able to safely take doses which might be dangerous or even fatal if taken by a nonuser. It is important to note that addiction exhibits a *tendency to increase the dose*. As will be seen, there is considerable dispute about whether this tendency is virtually unalterable or whether it is possible for some addicts to be maintained on a stabilized dose.

Once tolerance to opiates reaches a certain level, a distinct physiological (as well as psychological) dependence on the drug is produced. When this dependence has developed addiction is complete and the user is properly referred to as an addict (although the term *addict* sometimes has been used more broadly to cover regular use even of nondependence-producing drugs). The user's bodily system now, in effect, requires the drug to function smoothly, and if it is withdrawn the addict experiences acute symptoms of distress, known as the "abstinence syndrome." This syndrome includes a variety of both somatic and psychological symptoms, the severity of which is directly related to "the nature of the narcotic, the daily dosage used and the intervals, the duration of the addiction, the rapidity with which the drug is withdrawn, and the intensity of psychic and somatic dependence. It is inversely related to the resistance, vigor, and well-being of the addict." As this same report notes, despite the likely variations just indicated, "all recent authorities agree that the withdrawal syndrome has an organic basis." [10] It also seems clear that withdrawal of the confirmed addict from drugs is always at least an extremely unpleasant experience. Although in some cases the physical symptoms (which reflect disturbances of the neuromuscular, gastrointestinal, and respiratory systems) may be no more severe than a bad case of the flu,[11] in other instances the addict may be acutely and violently ill. And the psychological impact of the experience should not be overlooked:

I thought I would go mad. I was on the verge of insanity. I prayed for help, for relief, for death. My clothes must have been wet with sweat. I cursed the habit. If anyone could have seen me they would have thought I was a raving maniac.[12]

The phenomena of physical dependence and withdrawal distress are important to an understanding of the addiction problem. However, it would be a mistake to think that physical dependence fully explains the confirmed addict's need for drugs. Any individual administered opiates in sufficient dosages over a long enough time will, when administration is stopped, experience withdrawal distress. Thus many persons receiving such drugs in the course of medical treatment for the relief of pain become addicted to them. Yet not all such individuals revert to drugs after withdrawal. The term *drug addict* is ordinarily applied to those persons who, over some period of time, feel the "overpowering desire or need (compulsion)" mentioned in the WHO definition; a recent study has employed the term *craving* in discussing this important aspect of addiction.[13]

At the same time, the fact that the long-term addict has a physiological as well as psychological need for his drugs helps to put his condition and his behavior in proper perspective. Dependence also provides a basis for distinguishing truly addictive drugs from those which may be said to be only habit-forming—or to which users ordinarily develop merely a psychological habituation or dependence. Tobacco and coffee would be good examples of such habituating drugs. Stimulants such as cocaine, marihuana, and peyote (mescaline and LSD are similar) may produce striking effects on the users and sometimes strong psychological habituation, but they are not truly addicting. Amphetamines (such as Benzedrine) also fall into this category. Barbiturate drugs can, in prolonged use, lead to actual tolerance and physical dependence, but despite the danger of such addiction the medical use of barbiturates (primarily to treat insomnia) is widespread and socially approved in our society. Similarly, social approval of alcohol exists in the face of the well-known dangers of excessive drinking. Many experts insist that the condition of alcoholism is far more harmful to the individual than is opiate addiction. The unhappy lessons of the Prohibition experiment point up the key role negative social sanctions on drug use may play in creating secondary problems.

Causes of Addiction

According to a large body of psychological and psychoanalytic literature, addiction is but a symptom of an underlying psychic disorder, and certain types of individuals are psychologically predisposed to drug addiction. Despite variations reflecting different schools of psychological theory, psychologists and psychiatrists seem to agree on one central point—that the personality type typically exhibited by addicts involves strong dependency needs and pronounced feelings of inadequacy.[14]

Sociologist Alfred Lindesmith, who highlighted the popular misconceptions embodied in the "dope fiend" myth, also provided a detailed critique of the psychiatric approach to addiction. He was especially disturbed by the prevalent diagnosis of the addict as a "psychopathic personality" or as a person with "psychopathic diathesis or predisposition." One early and influential report, for example, had found that 86 per cent of the addicts studied had been affected "with some forms of nervous instability before they became addicted" . . . the largest category comprising "care-free individuals, devoted to pleasure, seeking new excitements and sensations, and usually having some ill-defined instability of personality that often expresses itself in mild infractions of social customs." [15] Lindesmith insisted that an inordinate emphasis was being placed upon the gratification the addict supposedly received from drugs and insufficient attention paid to his need to avoid withdrawal distress. His basic criticism, though, was that the psychiatric approach failed to develop a specific, self-consistent, and universally applicable theory of addiction. It evaded the problem of explaining how some psychologically "normal" persons (14 per cent in the study cited) become addicted. Nor did it explain cross-cultural and group variations in addiction rates. Early diagnostic studies, furthermore, made no use of control groups of nonaddicts, so a finding that 86 per cent of the addicts were psychologically disturbed could not really be evaluated. Even the use of control groups, however, would not remove the objection that the psychologists used as subjects only those who were already addicted—and in many cases, for many years. Such studies do not distinguish those traits which were the result of addiction from those which had caused it. Finally, Lindesmith contended, the very fact of addiction led the psychiatrist to find some underlying psychic difficulty. He noted the apparent tendency of psychiatrists to treat almost any trait exhibited by an addict as a possible indication of psychopathology. Thus some cases of addiction were held to be caused by lack of self-confidence; others by the pleasure-seeking drive of carefree individuals. He concluded: "The addict is evidently judged in advance. He is damned if he is self-confident and he is damned if he is not." [16]

On the basis of his own extensive interviews with addicts, Lindesmith developed what is perhaps the only distinctly sociological theory of addiction. He took as his goal an explanation that would include all cases, on the assumption that the only true causal explanation is one that is applicable to all instances of the phenomenon being explained. (This approach is rather different from that employed in most sociological research, where association between variables usually is stated in terms of probability—that is, statements are made about the likelihood of certain events, based on statistical outcomes in past observation.) Lindesmith began his research with a working hypothesis, which he revised to take account of negative cases wherever he encountered them. His final thesis, to which no exceptions could be found, was that "the knowledge or ignorance of the meaning of withdrawal distress and the use of opiates thereafter determines whether or not the individual becomes addicted." [17] (This refers to the persistence of a craving for the drug after withdrawal; continued use may result in physical dependence, regardless of the presence of this knowledge.) Essentially what this explanation provides is a retrospective description of the learning process through which all addicts go. A major criticism of the theory has been that it does not afford a basis for predicting which particular individuals will become addicted. Although this criticism seems partly warranted, Lindesmith's thesis has the merit of calling attention to the important element of learning involved in becoming an addict, and of suggesting that anyone could be susceptible to such a learning experience. (As another writer notes, in the current American drug situation this learning process involves not only knowledge of withdrawal and dependence but also important changes in the individual's over-all self-concept, gradual preoccupation with the need to obtain drug supplies, and likely involvement in a drug-addict subculture.[18]) Howard S. Becker's processual analysis of marihuana use has described the way in which, with that drug too, one learns to become an habitual user.[19]

Another approach to the causes of addiction lies in the extensive findings from research into the nature, extent, and distribution (spatial and social) of narcotics use in various large metropolitan centers. These area studies derive, in part, from the ecological approach developed some years ago by the Chicago school of sociologists. Indeed, it had already been found by Faris and Dunham in their classic study, *Mental Disorders in Urban Areas* (1939),[20] that in Chicago at that time addicts were highly concentrated in the deteriorating and generally disorganized "zone in transition" near the center of the city. Recent studies in New York, Chicago, Detroit, and other large cities show a persistent and clear relationship between ecological structure and the distribution of known addicts. Addiction is invariably found to be concentrated in those areas of the city that are most dilapidated and overcrowded, inhabited by persons of low socioeconomic and minority-group status, and characterized by high rates of other types of social pathology. One writer notes: "Such ecological studies of drug-users known to courts and hospitals reveal a higher degree of concentration of teen-age drug-users than is found for almost any other type of psychological or social problem." [21] This type of research has also disclosed the emergence in the larger metropolitan areas of a distinctive addict subculture.

A recent report has summarized the large body of data obtained in a ten-year study of juvenile drug use in New York, undertaken by the Research Center for Human Relations at New York University. This research, conducted under the guidance of social psychologists, combined an interest in the dynamic psychology of the individual deviant with an awareness of the importance of the socioeconomic and even legal aspects of the drug problem. The findings indicated that the areas with the highest drug use were those that were most overcrowded, had the highest poverty rates, and were populated largely by minority group members.[22] Not only was drug use found to be correlated with significant socioeconomic variables of that sort, but the New York researchers also concluded from an attitude survey that the high-use neighborhoods were characterized by a cultural climate conducive to experimentation with drugs. (They found a pervasive outlook on life which might be summarized as pessimistic antisocial hedonism.[23])

A major theoretical problem for such studies is posed by the fact that not all individuals in the areas of addict concentration take up drugs or even orient themselves to this dominant cultural climate. In seeking to explain the nonusers in high-use neighborhoods, Chein and his associates revert in some degree to a psychological-predisposition approach. They note certain functions the use of drugs may serve—such as relieving various personal and interpersonal strains and in general "establishing distance from the real-life demands of young adulthood." [24] A comparison of the family backgrounds of a group of addicts with those of a group of nonaddicts suggested that such background might constitute the basis for susceptibility to addiction. The unstable and disharmonious family milieux in which the addicts were reared contributed, they felt, to "the development of weak ego functioning, defective superego, inadequate masculine identification, lack of realistic levels of aspiration with respect to long-range goals, and a distrust of major social institutions." They also found that the fathers of the addicts had either been absent much of the time or were themselves highly disturbed or deviant.[25]

LIMITS OF THE CAUSAL APPROACH

These findings may suggest some of the practical limitations of past and present studies of causes of addiction. It is not too difficult to summarize these findings in a very general way. To begin with, it is now known that there is no single "type" among addicts—the physician who succumbs to addiction, for instance, is a quite different type sociologically (and perhaps psychologically) from the poverty-stricken minority-group member enmeshed in a delinquent and addict subculture. However, individuals in certain socioeconomic categories run a relatively greater risk of encountering and using narcotics than do those in other categories. Also, it seems likely that of those individuals in the high-risk categories it is the more troubled or the more disadvantaged, situationally, who are especially likely to take up drugs. (Although in another sense they could be viewed simply as those most fully socialized into the prevailing, if deviant, pattern.) The specific policy implications stemming from conclusions of this sort are not very clear. On the one hand it seems that addiction is partly caused by other general social disorders and that one way to deal with it is to attack the various socioeconomic ills which constitute the breeding ground of drug use. Similarly, various types of family life are highlighted as being detrimental, and presumably measures should be taken (assuming it could be determined just how this might be done) to improve the quality of interparent and parent-child relations. And if those individuals who do become addicted have certain personality problems, some kind of therapy or counselling should be aimed at treating the addicts themselves.

It seems clear that pursuit of all these types of treatment is desirable. At the same time, in the absence of any theoretical or therapeutic breakthrough that could be expected to result in a high rate of prevention or "cure" (the relapse rate in addiction cases is extremely high), it may be useful to approach the question of addiction in a somewhat different way. Whatever the causes of individual cases of addiction, the broader dimensions of the addiction problem may be amenable to improvement through variations in public policy. As one expert has stated:

> The prevalence and consequences of addiction in any society depend as much upon the social and legal definitions placed upon the non-medical use of narcotics as upon the nature and effects of narcotics or the nature of the persons who become addicted.[26]

To some observers, attempted reforms of the legal policies on addiction never reach the core of the problem. Indeed most psychologically oriented students of addiction maintain that, without

individual treatment, persons succumbing to addiction would—
even in the absence of drugs—be involved in some kind of problem-
atic behavior. Yet few responsible students of the problem view
psychological treatment of susceptible individuals as offering a
complete solution of the addiction problem. Attention to narrowly
defined causes cannot lead to a full understanding of addiction as
a social problem. Such an understanding requires consideration of
the legal policies which define and seek to control that problem.

Drug Laws and Enforcement

NARCOTICS LEGISLATION

The practical effect of American narcotics laws is to define the
addict as a criminal offender. This result has stemmed largely from
the interpretation given the Harrison Act passed by Congress in
1914. This law requires registration of all legitimate drug-handlers
and payment of a special tax on drug transactions. It thus establishes
a licensing system for the control of legitimate domestic drug traffic.
In this respect the Harrison Act has been extremely successful, and
it seems clear that originally the statute was intended merely to
serve this function. It specifically provided that the restrictions
would not apply to dispensing of narcotics to a patient by a physician
"in the course of his professional practice" and "for legitimate
medical purposes." As a recent and authoritative report concludes:
"Clearly, it was not the intention of Congress that government
should interfere with medical treatment of addicts." [27] Yet, through
a combination of restrictive regulations, attention only to favorable
court decisions, and harassment, the Narcotics Division of the U.S.
Treasury Department (and its successor, the Federal Bureau of
Narcotics) has effectively and severely limited the freedom of medical
practitioners to treat addict-patients as they see fit—in particular, to
provide addicts with drugs when that is believed medically advisable.

An early test of the Act came in 1919 (*Webb v. U.S.*). The facts showed flagrant abuse of the law by the defendant, Dr. Webb, who had sold thousands of narcotics prescriptions indiscriminately, for fifty cents apiece. The government, however, presented the issue to the U.S. Supreme Court in the following form:

> If a practicing and registered physician issues an order for mor-phine to an habitual user thereof, the order not being issued by him in the course of professional treatment in the attempted cure of the habit, but being issued for the purpose of providing the user with morphine sufficient to keep him comfortable by maintaining his customary use, is such order a physician's prescription [under the specific exemption in the Act]?

Accepting this restrictive definition of "professional treatment," the Court asserted that "to call such an order for the use of morphine a physician's prescription would be so plain a perversion of meaning that no discussion of the subject is required." [28] Another case three years later (*U.S. v. Behrman*) also involved obvious abuse of the Harrison Act; here the doctor had given to an addict a huge quantity of narcotics for use as he (the addict) saw fit. In what one student of these decisions[29] has termed a "trick indictment," the government glossed over the doctor's quite evident bad faith, acted as though the drugs had been provided in good faith for the purpose of treating the addict, and obtained a ruling to the effect that any such whole-sale prescriptions (in good faith or not) violated the law. At the same time, however, the court indicated that the prescription of a single dose or even a number of doses—made in good faith—would not be punishable under the Act.[30]

To this day, the Federal Bureau of Narcotics quotes with approval the *Webb* and *Behrman* decisions, making little or no mention of an important 1925 ruling (*Linder v. U.S.*) which would seem to challenge and greatly limit these earlier judgments. In the 1925 case, the government prosecuted a well-established Spokane physician who had prescribed a small amount of narcotics for a patient who was actually an agent of the Bureau. (The defendant claimed that the "patient" had said she was in great pain from a stomach ailment and that her regular physician was out of town; she claimed that she had said she was an addict). In a unanimous opinion, the Supreme Court reversed Dr. Linder's conviction, stating:

> The enactment under consideration . . . says nothing of 'addicts' and does not undertake to prescribe methods for their medical treatment. They are diseased and proper subjects for such treatment, and we cannot possibly conclude that a physician acted improperly or unwisely or for other than medical purpose solely because he has dispensed to one of them, in the ordinary course, and in good faith, four small tablets of morphine or cocaine for relief of conditions incident to addiction.

The Court also specifically held that the *Webb* and *Behrman* rulings should not be extended beyond the facts in those particular cases.[31]

The acceptance of medical discretion embodied in this decision has in no way been reflected in federal narcotics regulations:

> An order purporting to be a prescription issued to an addict or habitual user of narcotics, not in the course of professional treatment but for the purpose of providing the user with narcotics sufficient to keep him comfortable by maintaining his customary use, is not a prescription within the meaning and intent of the act; and the person filling such an order, as well as the person issuing it, may be charged with violation of the law.[32]

The *Linder* decision did not prevent the Bureau of Narcotics from carrying out what a recent account has termed a "persecution of the physicians"; at least during the period 1925-38 there were numerous prosecutions and convictions of physicians for narcotics violations.[33] There are probably few such cases today, partly because doctors have been so effectively cowed by the early prosecutions and stringent regulations.

The Bureau of Narcotics insists that it does not attempt to interfere with legitimate medical practice. Yet the physician's position remains tenuous. As a joint committee of the American Bar Association and the American Medical Association has noted, a physician's prescription of drugs for an addict will probably be upheld if it is in "good faith" and if he adheres to "proper medical standards." But these very questions can only be determined in the course of an actual court trial of a specific case:

> The physician has no way of knowing *before* he attempts to treat, and/or prescribe drugs to an addict, whether his activities will be condemned or condoned. He does not have any criteria or standards to guide him in dealing with drug addicts, since what constitutes bona fide medical practice and good faith depends upon the facts and circumstances of each case. . . .[34]

Over the years the Harrison Act has been supplemented by many other antinarcotics statutes under which the unauthorized possession, sale, or transfer of drugs is severely punished. Rather than constituting a rationally planned program for dealing with the narcotics problem, this legislation has mainly represented an emotional response to periodic crises. For example, public concern about narcotics—aroused by the Kefauver Committee's 1951 investigation of organized crime—resulted in a federal law (the Boggs Act) imposing severe mandatory minimum sentences for narcotics offenses.[35] Another congressional investigation four years later, focusing entirely on the drug traffic, led to the enactment of the Narcotic Control Act of 1956, which raised the minimum sentences for offenders and which permits the death penalty for those who sell narcotics to persons under eighteen.[36] In addition to the federal statutes, the various states have enacted their own antinarcotics laws.[37]

Many observers, including some prominent jurists, have condemned the harsh penalties imposed by recent drug laws—objecting particularly to the fact that such statutes typically draw no distinction between the nonaddict peddler and the addict. Illustrating these objections was the 1956 statement of Robert Meyner, former governor of New Jersey, vetoing a bill which would have increased mandatory minimum sentences for narcotics violators and barred suspended sentences and probation even for first offenders. Stating that he would have unhesitatingly approved if such penalties applied only to nonaddicted suppliers of drugs, Meyner noted:

> . . . although the deterrent quality of punishment may be conceded in certain areas, the question remains whether deterrence may not

also be achieved by severe sentences where the facts so warrant, without the inherent self-defeating weakness of laws which are excessively severe in cases involving individuals whose offenses do not merit the punishment commanded by the bills. . . .[38]

THE FAILURE OF ENFORCEMENT

What have these legal policies accomplished? Law enforcement officials often assert that addiction is being kept under control, yet even government estimates have placed the number of addicts between 45,000 and 60,000, and almost all nongovernmental experts feel these figures greatly understate the problem. In any case, it is certain that these laws have not come anywhere close to eliminating addiction. They have, however, greatly influenced the narcotics problem. Cut off from legal supplies of narcotics, the addict naturally seeks illicit drug sources. The strong demand of addicts for their drugs means that there are huge profits to be made in the black market, and this in turn makes the risks involved in such an endeavor worthwhile. According to one account, the retail value of one thousand dollars worth of heroin may surpass three million dollars.[39] It is understandable, then, that the endless circle of supply and demand alluded to in the discussion of abortion should also be in evidence here. The addict's position in this exchange is so vulnerable that not only must he pay exorbitant amounts but typically he must settle for a highly diluted product; the repeated adulteration of narcotics as they go down the line from the original importer to the various distributors and ultimately to the addict is well-known. Many experts contend that no amount of law enforcement effort could reasonably be expected to stifle the black market in narcotics. Such observers believe that, given the extreme and continuous demand of addicts, some way always will be found to make the drugs available illegally. For, as Robert Merton has suggested: "In strictly economic terms, there is no relevant difference between the provision of licit and of illicit goods and services." [40]

Most enforcement officials admit that the task of significantly curbing the smuggling of narcotics into the country is a pretty hopeless task. The former U.S. Commissioner of Narcotics himself has been quoted as saying that the combined efforts of the Army, the

Navy, the Narcotics Bureau and the FBI could not eliminate drug smuggling. As a customs agent has pointed out, discussing his agency's operations in New York City:

> On normal passenger arrival days it is the policy of the collector of customs at the Port of New York to examine baggage 100 per cent, but when the passenger arrivals are heavy, a spot-check of baggage is performed. Under these circumstances it is not difficult to understand how a passenger using a false-bottom trunk or a suitcase with a false compartment might be able to conceal narcotics and get by the examining inspector; searches of persons are infrequently made and then only as a last resort and only based on substantial reasons.[41]

Again, as in the case of abortion, there occurs the competitive development of enforcement and antienforcement techniques.

But, basically, it is the supply-and-demand element and the lack of a complaining victim, rather than the cleverness of the law violators, that render the drug laws so largely unenforceable. Predictably in such a situation law enforcers must resort to special investigative techniques. A major source of evidence in narcotics cases is the addict-informer. Though the addict-informer faces grave danger of underworld reprisal, their eagerness to stay out of jail (and avoid sudden withdrawal from drugs) or simply their need for funds with which to purchase drugs impels many addicts to assume this role. The Bureau of Narcotics is authorized to pay the "operating expenses" of informants whose information leads to the seizure of drugs in illicit traffic; hence, the Bureau at least indirectly supports the addiction (and the "crime") of some addicts in order to uncover others. Despite this fact, and the questionable legal aspects involved in trapping suspects through informers, enforcement spokesmen insist on the propriety and even the necessity of such practices. According to two enforcement experts:

> The police officer who by methodical planning, supplemented sometimes by happy accident, is able to set up and maintain listening posts in the underworld, represents one of the finest professional developments in the unceasing war of organized society against underworld forces.[42]

Often the informer or even the narcotics agent himself will directly attempt to obtain a prescription or a supply of drugs from a suspected doctor or peddler or through an addict. Thus narcotics investigations frequently tread the fine line between detection and entrapment. As in the case of antihomosexuality operations, the courts will not uphold prosecutions based on acts or statements directly planned or instigated by enforcement officers. There is even the danger that enforcement activities may hinder attempts by addicts to curb their addiction:

> The case at bar illustrates an evil which the defense of entrapment is designed to overcome. The government informer entices someone attempting to avoid narcotics not only into carrying out an illegal sale but also into returning to the habit of use. Selecting the proper time, the informer then tells the government agent. The set-up is accepted by the agent without even a question as to the manner in which the informer encountered the seller. Thus the government plays on the weaknesses of an innocent party and beguiles him into committing crimes which he otherwise would not have attempted. Law enforcement does not require methods such as this.[43]

The use of informers and agent-decoys are not the only unpalatable police techniques used to combat the drug traffic. Perhaps more than any other category, narcotics cases have notoriously given rise to grave issues of constitutional law—as witnessed by major U.S. Supreme Court decisions dealing with alleged infringements of suspects' constitutional safeguards against improper arrest, illegal search and seizure, self-incrimination, and the like. One of the best-known of these decisions was in the case of *Rochin v. California* (1952). There the police, suspecting the defendant of dealing in narcotics, illegally broke into his room. During the course of a struggle with the intruding officers, the suspect managed to swallow two small objects which the officers had attempted to seize from a table near the suspect's bed. The police then rushed him to a hospital, where—despite his protests—a physician pumped his stomach. As a result, the investigators found morphine which was later used as evidence against him on a narcotics charge. The Supreme Court held unanimously that conviction on the basis of such evidence violated due process of law. Writing for the Court, Justice Frankfurter stated:

> . . . the proceedings by which this conviction was obtained do more than offend some fastidious squeamishness or private sentimentalism about combatting crime too energetically. This is conduct that shocks the conscience. Illegally breaking into the privacy of the petitioner, the struggle to open his mouth and remove what was there, the forcible extraction of his stomach's contents—this course of proceeding by agents of government to obtain evidence is bound to offend even hardened sensibilities. They are methods too close to the rack and the screw to permit of constitutional differentiation.[44]

In addition to the questionable nature of enforcement activities, the efforts required to obtain evidence in narcotics cases may lead to an unwarranted expenditure of police energies (and hence, indirectly, of taxpayers' money). In one case five detectives spent a month in Greenwich Village disguised as "beatniks"; one was reported even to have achieved a slight reputation as a poet. According to a news account the entire New York police narcotics squad (then numbering 140 men and women) participated in resulting arrests.[45] If such efforts led to the conviction of leading figures in the drug traffic, they might be worthwhile. Yet it is widely known that current enforcement activities more often serve to ensnare minor violators. The American drug traffic involves at least four classes of sellers: importers, (rarely addicts themselves), professional wholesalers (also rarely addicts), peddlers (who may be addicted), and pushers (addicts who sell to get funds for their own drug supplies). As numerous commentators have noted, it is the addicts, pushers, and perhaps some peddlers who are most affected by antinarcotics enforcement. The Bureau of Narcotics and other government agencies protest that they have in fact managed to convict some of the major figures in the illegal drug traffic. But, as Judge John Murtagh has pointed out:

> The Bureau itself admits that there is a new dope ring to take the place of every one it smashes and that periodic round-ups, even if conducted on a national scale, while they may serve to weaken the racket never effect a killing blow. Perhaps the biggest round-up in American history was that staged in 1952 . . . which netted a total of

nearly five hundred suspects. But was the syndicate affected by this round-up? Hardly at all.[46]

In short, it is evident that the police face an impossible task in seeking to enforce current drug laws. The laws are inherently self-defeating. Even to approximate efficiency in their administration would require the wholesale violation of legal rights, which the courts will not permit. Likewise, judges are often unwilling to impose maximum sentences on addicted drug violators, and even prosecutors sometimes proceed against them under the less stringent of several possible charges. At the same time, enforcement personnel are under considerable pressure from segments of the public and from higher officials to produce results. It is not surprising, under these circumstances, that they exhibit strong hostility toward the addict, and view themselves as engaged in a "war" against addiction. With a sharp attitudinal dividing line separating the "good guys" (law enforcers) from the "bad guys" (those involved in the world of drugs), important distinctions such as that between the addict and the nonaddicted drug violator, blur or disappear.[47] These punitive attitudes, in turn, lead to increasingly brutal treatment of the addict, without any corresponding increase in the effectiveness of antinarcotics measures.

Addict Crime and Subculture

These laws do not merely fail to curb addiction, they also vitally influence addict behavior. The issue of crime by addicts has long concerned students of addiction. (The criminal behavior being considered here, of course, is not the mere possession and use of drugs— which may or may not be defined as criminal.) One point alluded to at the beginning of this chapter must be underscored here: there is no evidence suggesting that crime results from the direct effects of the drugs themselves. Also, the addict is much more likely to commit nonviolent crimes against property than violent crimes against persons. This is to be expected from the depressant nature of the drugs. In an early study, psychiatrist Lawrence Kolb suggested even that "one is led to believe violent crime could be much less prevalent if all habitual criminals were addicts who could obtain sufficient morphine or heroin to keep themselves fully charged with one of these drugs at all times." [48] There is strong evidence that most crimes committed by addicts are undertaken in order to obtain funds with which to purchase illicit drugs. The statements and records of individual addicts amply corroborate the relationship between drug use and "crime for profit." Furthermore, the New York studies have shown that in high drug-use areas there are relatively high rates of cash-producing delinquencies (robbery, burglary, procuring, and the like) and relatively low rates of violent crimes and other nonprofit offenses.[49] Similarly, a study of arrest data for Chicago in 1951 (comparing cases handled in the Narcotic Bureau with those processed by the municipal police department) indicated that "the number of arrests for nonviolent property crimes was proportionately higher among addicts. In contrast, however, the number of arrests of addicts for violent offenses against the person, such as rape and aggravated assault, was only a fraction of the proportion constituted by such arrests among the population at large." [50]

A recurrent issue with respect to addict criminality has been whether addicts have criminal records antedating their addiction. Pescor, in a 1936-37 study of the records of over a thousand addict-patients admitted to the Lexington, Kentucky, U.S. Public Health Service Hospital, found that a substantial majority were not antisocial prior to addiction.[51] In recent years, however, the Bureau of Narcotics has contended that most American addicts were involved in criminal activities prior to becoming addicted. Because drug use is concentrated in neighborhoods in which crime and delinquency also flourish, it is not surprising if there is some truth to this claim. But the most significant facts about addict-crime in the United States today seem to be that addiction reduces the inclination to engage in violent crime, and that persistent involvement in petty theft or prostitution (in order to support the drug habit) is an almost inevitable consequence of addiction. It is noteworthy that in Great Britain, where the addict usually can obtain needed drugs legally and at low cost, there is practically no crime associated with addiction. This is certainly in sharp contrast to the situation pointed up in the following statement by the Police Commissioner of New York City:

> The facts are that of our major crime arrests, about 7 per cent of the people arrested are addicts, users of drugs. We know many crimes are committed where no arrests are made, or an arrest is made after several crimes have been committed by the same person . . . probably three times that 7 per cent—21 to 25 per cent of all crime results from the necessity to maintain the habit. This is particularly true in prostitution and petty larceny.[52]

Another apparent consequence of the illegality of narcotics is the expansion of, and immersion of most addicts in, a specialized addict subculture. Cohen's statement (*see* p. 85) of the conditions necessary for the emergence of a subculture included the effective interaction of a number of persons with similar problems of adjustment. In drug addiction, as in homosexuality, this condition is present. It has been argued that the addict benefits psychologically from knowledge of and contact with others who share his plight. Furthermore, certain forms of subculture which develop among addicts might exist even if drug use were not an important part of their lives. This reasoning is in line with the belief that a particular cultural climate underlies drug use and is also suggested by Harold Finestone's analysis of the "cool cat" pattern found among young male Negro addicts in Chicago.[53] Because all reports on known drug-users in the United States indicate that young male Negroes are highly overrepresented, this particular study may be of special importance.

The drug-users interviewed by Finestone varied, of course, but a dominant type emerged: these addicts had developed a way of life through which they could conceive of themselves as belonging to an elite group, a society of "cool cats." The "cat" tended to be a sharp dresser, a smooth talker, and a clever manipulator—someone who could stay "cool" in the face of difficulties. He viewed himself as an operator, and in general held "squares" in contempt. His relations with women tended to be exploitative, sometimes leading the "cat" into pimping or at least into admiration of the pimp role. The "cat" prided himself on getting by without working, and each "cat" had some "hustle"—a nonwork way of "making some bread" (obtaining money). Every cat also had his "kick"—and the appeal of heroin was that it provided the ultimate kick. In short,

> The "cat" seeks through a harmonious combination of charm, ingratiating speech, dress, music, the proper dedication to his "kick," and unrestrained generosity to make of his day-to-day life a gracious work of art. Everything is to be pleasant and everything he does and values is to contribute to a cultivated aesthetic approach to living. The "cool cat" exemplifies all of these elements in proper balance. He demonstrates his ability to "play it cool" in his unruffled manner of dealing with outsiders such as the police, and in the self-assurance with which he confronts emergencies in the society of "cats." Moreover, the "cat" feels himself to be any man's equal. He is convinced that he can go anywhere and mingle easily with anyone. . . .[54]

Finestone's interpretation of the factors underlying this pattern highlights elements that would pertain even in the absence of addiction, and in fact he states that the basic features of the "cats'" orientation very likely preceded their introduction to heroin. He suggests that "the 'cat' as a social type is the personal counterpart of an expressive social movement," and states that this phenomenon must be viewed in the broader context of the social segregation and discrimination experienced by these Negro youths. The "cat" may represent one type of adaptation to the various frustrations felt by this group, one attempt to develop a separate social system in which security and status can be achieved—while repudiating the norms and values of the discriminators (the larger society). Finestone also notes that some features of this way of life (such as concern with dress, music, language, and pleasure-seeking) are characteristic of the adolescent world generally. But in addition to the typical problems of adolescence, the "cat" is "confronted by a special set of problems of color, tradition, and identity."

REPRESSION BREEDS SUBCULTURE

Addict subculture also reflects the pressures produced by anti-addiction policies. That is brought out in an analysis of addict life prepared by Seymour Fiddle, a sociologist working with the East Harlem Protestant Parish in New York:

> While certain patterns of addict life may have been in existence before the Harrison Act, the conversion of addiction into a mass criminal activity appears to have given special form and meaning to addiction, so that we may speak reasonably about an addict culture operating as a system.[55]

Fiddle cites the existence of two major aspects of this subculture: the "circulatory system" and the "survival system." The former term refers to the system of roles and interrelationships through which addicts secure illegal drugs. With the exception of physician-addicts and some other well-to-do addicts who may obtain narcotics (illegally, but with slight risk) from "legitimate" sources (such as doctors and pharmacists), all addicts in the United States must enter into the complex underworld network distributing illicit drugs. The addict, then, is of necessity thrown into contact with drug peddlers or pushers, he may very likely become a pusher himself in order to support his habit, he invariably comes to engage in frequent interaction with other drug-users as well as with distributors. It is to his practical as well as psychological advantage to engage himself in every aspect of the drug-distributing and drug-consuming world. Fiddle makes this clear in discussing key features and functions of the "survival system," which he lists as follows: (1) ideology of justification; (2) the "reproductive" process; (3) defensive communication; (4) neighborhood warning systems; (5) ritualistic, magical and cyclical patterns; and (6) the attractiveness of personal relations.[56]

Like other oppressed minorities, drug addicts adopt a justifying ideology to support their morale and lessen their feeling of isolation. Although this might be true even in the absence of legal repression, it is all the more important in the face of such repression. By *"reproductive" process,* Fiddle refers to the fact that the system continually requires new members in order to maintain itself. The considerable involvement of addicts in the drug-distribution process has led some observers to assert that it is basically the addicts themselves who spread the habit, and that therefore elimination of the "professional" peddler would not appreciably alter the problem of

ddiction. In this view, the subculture and the addict-pusher are
een almost as causes of the addiction problem. Yet the evidence indicates that they are at least partly caused, in turn, by the supply-
demand cycle and the pattern of legal repression. In any case, it is
obvious that behind whatever distribution addicts themselves engage
in are professional illicit suppliers who are motivated solely by the
desire for profit. As one addict has put it: "The trail always leads
back to the same direction, to the peddler who was originally around
to turn somebody on [introduce him to drug-taking]. . . .[57]

Addict argot and special speech and gestural habits may serve
practical as well as morale-enhancing functions. The need for
cohesive ties in the face of strong adverse reaction is especially
conducive to the development of such argot among deviants. But
defensive communication means more than just a special addict
jargon. Another aspect is the "grapevine system":

> Information about the coming of the police, or about the kind of
> heroin being sold, in different parts of the city, are said to pass rapidly
> and accurately, with what is said to be greater safety than that fur-
> nished by the telephone. . . . Information is sifted out according to a
> consensus concerning the reliability of different individuals. In par-
> ticular, there is a belief that informers can be spotted so that they can
> be excluded from the grapevine or sent onto a fake grapevine. In
> some periods, information can be so valuable that it is paid for by the
> addicted.[58]

It is also reported that in some neighborhoods (particularly where
there is an ethnic or other communal bond) even nonaddicts may be
more or less willing to protect addicts from police interference.
Despite the usually strained relations between addicts and their
nonaddicted neighbors, "a residue of loyalty may continue to keep
the local populace from any active cooperation with the police." As
part of the "ritual, magical, and cyclical patterns" Fiddle discusses
the addict's use of time—which reflects the bondage of addiction and
the need for addicts in our society to devote almost all their energy
to the search for illicit supplies:

> There is a time, or some time, for getting money; a time, or some
> time, for getting drugs; a time, or some time, for using the drugs.

(An interesting point is the way in which the term *scoring* [purchasing] has been inflated to cover all phases of the process.) This triadic pattern may be repeated several times a day, or may be abbreviated according to the skill and fortunes of the addicted person. But whatever the combination, the day is ordered according to a detectable perspective.

Through police intervention this perspective may well lose its clarity, so that the day is increasingly freighted with despair, bitterness, and confusion. These experiences themselves act as secondary sources for drug use as the drug is called upon to perform sedative functions. . . .[59]

Finally Fiddle notes that addict "life" serves a general function (presumably more psychological than practical or defensive) in fostering intense interpersonal relationships between addicted individuals.

It should not be thought that the addict subculture engulfs everyone coming into contact with it. In all high drug-use neighborhoods nonusing "squares" live alongside the addicts. Although drug distribution is closely related to the underworld, delinquent gangs as such are not a key factor in the promotion of addiction. In New York it was found that although some gangs provided "an arena in which the use of narcotics can develop," generally the gangs not only discouraged and inhibited drug use but also satisfied needs "which may otherwise lead to earlier use. . . ." [60] Another type of misapprehension about the addict subculture may be inadvertently created by "inside" accounts of addict life in America. It is not true that addiction to narcotics automatically makes the individual a member of an addict subculture. This is shown, for example, by one study of American physician-addicts. Those interviewed "almost never associated with other physician-addicts, or did not do so knowingly. They did not have any occasion for doing so, either for the purpose of getting drugs or for passing time, or for emotional support." [61] As might be expected, it was similarly found that the physicians in question did not make use of the special addict jargon. Thus, although there may be some psychological pressures working to bring addicts together, the addict's over-all social and legal status and his relation to drug sources seem to be the overriding factors determining subcultural membership. This point is borne out by

he experience in Britain, where the availability of drugs eliminates
le need for addicts to involve themselves in underworld distribution
rocesses and thus prevents the significant development of an addict
ubculture.

The gradual immersion of most American addicts in a world of
heir own is inextricably connected with the general process by
which they have been cast out of respectable society. The social
definition of the addict as a criminal not only vitally influences his
behavior but also significantly affects his self-image. Certainly the
knowledge that one has become fully addicted must in itself have a
profound impact on this self-image. At the same time it is noteworthy that although the physician-addict and the subcultural-type
addict are addicted in precisely the same physiological sense, their
elf-images are likely to be strikingly different. Both may recognize
hemselves as addicts, yet the physician is most unlikely to consider
himself a criminal. On the other hand, the addict who is driven to
underworld connections and to crime in order to support his habit
cannot help but begin to feel that he is an enemy of society (or at
east that society is *his* enemy). A self-fulfilling-prophecy cycle is set
n motion from which it is very difficult for such an addict to
extricate himself. He is aware that respectable people view him as a
criminal, and he sees that he is beginning to act like one.[62] Increasingly he must turn to the drug world for interpersonal support
as well as for drug supplies. As the need to finance his habit occupies
more and more of his time and energy, and as other worlds (such as
those of work, family, and so on) recede into the background or fade
away completely, addiction becomes a way of life.

Treatment

Attempts to deal with this extremely complex situation have
mainly involved the medical and psychiatric treatment of individual
addicts. It is not difficult, in a hospital setting and perhaps elsewhere,
gradually to withdraw the addict from drugs with a minimum of discomfort. Unfortunately this does not constitute a real cure, for the
key characteristic of the confirmed addict is the craving for the drug

which exists even when there is no physical dependence. Experts are agreed that various types of postwithdrawal assistance will usually be necessary if any real success is to be achieved.

Until recently most of the treatment of addicts in this country took place in the U.S. Public Health Service hospitals at Lexington, Kentucky, and at Fort Worth, Texas. With highly qualified staff and a comprehensive treatment program—including gradual withdrawal from drugs, vocational and recreational activity, and a limited amount of psychotherapy—these treatment centers have represented a well-intentioned effort to deal with the addict medically. However, most nongovernmental observers feel that the results have been far from satisfactory. To begin with, the federal hospitals, which accept both voluntary patients and some compulsory committals of addicted drug law violators, have a combined capacity of less than 2500. Recognition that such facilities are totally inadequate has led, in the last five years or so, to the establishment by several states and large cities of either special institutions or special units in general hospitals. It seems likely that more and better treatment facilities will become available in the near future.

But increasing the number and improving the quality of such facilities does not strike at the heart of the problem of treating addicts. Any treatment effort must come to grips with the disheartening phenomenon of probable relapse. Favorable estimates have placed the rate (for the major specialized-treatment institutions) at around 75 per cent; less optimistic estimates, at 90-95 per cent.[6] Such statistics reflect something more basic than the shortcomings of particular institutions; they illustrate the impossibility of overturning, by conventional medical procedures, what is often a way of life. On his return to the community, the treated addict faces many of the same sorts of difficulties experienced by the former convict: lack of understanding among relatives and nonaddict friends, inability to obtain a decent job, reinvolvement in the very cultural climate and interpersonal associations which may have led him into the deviance in the first place. These are all very real problems associated with relapse, and a comprehensive treatment program must seek to cope with them. But, in a broader sense, a complete reassessment of the individual's outlook on life and his view of his own goals and behavior may be necessary. It has been suggested that, after successful withdrawal, the former addict begins a running struggle with his problems of social identity. As the same writer goes on to state:

> The ex-addict who is successful in remaining abstinent relates to new groups of people, participates in their experience, and to some extent begins to evaluate the conduct of his former associates (and perhaps his own when he was an addict) in terms of the values of the new group.[64]

Even prolonged individual psychotherapy may be insufficient to produce this kind of transformation.

A COMMUNITY PROGRAM

A comprehensive program of action-research in the voluntary treatment of male addicts at New York City's Metropolitan Hospital has convinced psychiatrists involved in that project that "new types of therapeutic intervention" are needed, "and, above all, a public health approach with the emphasis on prevention of the disease." Experience there has indicated that the goals and orientations of standard psychotherapy tend to clash with the addict-patient's preoccupation with short-term situational problems; that the differences between the socioeconomic backgrounds and life experiences of therapist and those of the addict cause "serious communication and countertransference problems"; and that even medically trained therapists may exhibit considerable ambivalence regarding the program's objectives and techniques as well as in their general attitudes toward addicts and addiction.[65] The modest success of the program at Metropolitan Hospital has been largely the result of the attempt to relate treatment efforts to the addict's total situation in the local community—particularly through the development of a close working relationship with a neighborhood agency long occupied in assisting addicts. Out of this relationship have come regular referral of patients (all voluntary), continuous sharing of information about the drug situation, and a program under which psychiatrists from the treatment unit actually spend time at the agency seeing former and prospective patients and increasing their awareness of the addict subculture. The clergyman-director of this agency insists that "neighborhood-based referral and aftercare units are the most important of a number of parts in a total treatment program for the addicted." [66] Treatment-researchers at Metropolitan have outlined a "model continuum" for a total community-based addiction-treatment program. After the initial contact between the addict and the medical staff—which might occur at the hospital or in a cooperating neighborhood agency—there would be a period of ambulatory care "until there could be an effective referral to the in-patient facility for detoxification." Such out-patient care could take various forms: "The patient may enter a sheltered workshop program, may be placed on a pharmacological regime, or may be engaged in a form of interview treatment. . . ." Once the withdrawal from drugs has been accomplished, the patient would be admitted to a Day-Night Center, located away from but near the hospital. After an extended stay there, he would "return in gradual stages to his neighborhood under the continued supervision of a clinic which would be jointly operated by the hospital and the neighborhood agency." The patient would continue to receive varying forms of help from the treatment team "until rehabilitation and social integration were achieved." [67]

Such a program does not directly solve the problem of establishing socially constructive neighborhood values and institutions into which the treated addict can be "integrated," but it does represent an effort to relate individual care to the neighborhood setting. A similar, if more modest, attempt to link institutional therapy with readjustment to the community is seen in the establishment of "halfway houses" in which addicts released from treatment institutions can reside prior to complete reinvolvement in the community at large. Because under current laws the institutionalization many addicts undergo is in prisons or prison-like treatment centers, this scheme may have special value. Gradual introduction to outside life, group and individual counselling, vocational guidance, and general support may be provided in such a setting. On the other hand, compulsory assignment to such a program, especially when the program maintains direct links with the formal administration of correctional institutions, may partly undermine its effectiveness. [68]

SYNANON HOUSE

A more direct attack on the addict's probable commitment to a deviant value system and way of life has been the program of Synanon House. Under this program former addicts live with and work with current ones—withdrawing them from drugs and attempting gradually to win them over (through group discussion and other techniques) to antidrug attitudes and positive social goals. Although available statistics are meager, it does appear that Synanon has been effective in keeping a substantial number of former addicts off drugs for prolonged periods. In analyzing the program's relative success observers have pointed to the insistence that each member voluntarily submit to the rules of an expressly antiaddiction group, the continuous indoctrination by the group in new attitudes and behavior patterns, the group cohesion which develops through common purpose and which is enhanced by the fact that the "reformers" are of the members' "own kind," and the program's system of work roles representing "stages of graded competence" in which the member works his way up to levels of increased responsibility and obtains a status quite different from that of mere inmate or even patient.[69]

One of the shortcomings of the program has been that, despite the plan that members should eventually work their way out of the system so that they are both living and working in the outside community, most members who have successfully abstained from drugs have in fact remained (vocationally as well as residentially) within the organization. This suggests limits on the extent to which Synanon can fully rehabilitate addicts (let alone solve the addiction problem). One writer, emphasizing these limitations, has suggested that actually members have substituted a dependence on Synanon for the dependence on drugs, and that the program should be seen as a protective community rather than a truly therapeutic community aimed at the eventual reintegration of the patient with the outside world.[70] Despite this shortcoming, Synanon seems to show considerable promise as a device for the voluntary treatment of at least some addicts. The program has encountered community protests in various locales when it has attempted to set up residential centers, but this has not prevented the establishment and apparently smooth operation of a number of Synanon houses.

KEY TREATMENT ISSUES

Most general discussions of the treatment of addiction have indicated dispute about three central and interrelated issues. The first involves institutional versus out-patient treatment. Experts generally agree that a hospital provides the most appropriate setting for the withdrawal of the addict from drugs. At the same time, some observers emphasize that specialized treatment facilities for addicts have certain drawbacks. One authority states: "My opinion, borne out by experience, is that any treatment center which brings active drug addicts together in large numbers is bound to fail of its purpose." [71] One addict's account of her stay in Lexington emphasized the fact that conversation among the patients was almost entirely about narcotics. Rather than being weaned away from the world of drugs, the patient may thus experience a strengthening and reinforcement of his identification with that world. As this girl went on to say, it was on release from Lexington that she became convinced she was an incurable addict: "I felt beaten when I got out of there, really beaten." [72] The very process of treatment, then, if it occurs in a compulsory context, may promote and reinforce the addict's deviant self-image.

Officially, American policy has sanctioned only institutional treatment of addicts. Out-patient treatment has persistently been repudiated in material distributed by the Bureau of Narcotics—which frequently cites a 1924 pronouncement of the American Medical Association opposing such treatment. Insistence on the need to hospitalize addicts may prevent useful exploration of other treatment approaches. One project in New York has indicated that some addicts can be successfully withdrawn on an out-patient basis, and suggested that the difficulties of dealing with addicts as voluntary out-patients have sometimes been exaggerated. The ability of this project to keep thirteen addicts in voluntary out-patient treatment for a full year was attributed to its nonpunitive and nonmoralizing orientation.[73]

Closely related to the out-patient-institutional dispute are strong differences of opinion about the value of compulsory treatment. Under present policies, most institutionalization of addicts is more or less compulsory. Addicts are directly committed by courts, given the option of commitment instead of prison, or else forced into treatment by the pressures of maintaining the drug habit illegally (for example, many addicts undergo withdrawal treatment in order that they can resume their drug use at a lower dosage level and hence at lower cost). The extremely high relapse rate has convinced some observers that compulsory treatment simply will not work. When the compulsion is blatant, it will make little difference that the institution is called a *treatment center* or *hospital,* and that the addict is labeled a *patient* rather than an *offender.* As Szasz and Goffman have suggested in their discussions of commitment to mental institutions, the facts of deprivation of liberty and of involuntary immersion in the life of a "total institution" will often overshadow in the committed individual's view any appreciation he might have of efforts by the treatment staff to help him.[74] This may be particularly true in the addict's case since ordinarily he will be fully capable of understanding just what is happening to him. In any case, apart from how the patient views a specific institutional program, there is the basic problem that without the addict's cooperation in a genuine effort at prolonged abstinence no cure can be expected. Although some therapists have stated that addict-patients require compulsion to help them develop the self-discipline necessary for a cure, others stress that the success of any treatment program has been the result of its voluntary character. They urge that it may be necessary to recognize that one simply cannot cure an addict, in the long term, against his will.

This brings up a third major issue in addiction treatment: are the terms *cure* and *treatment* synonymous? All specialists agree that addiction is undesirable and that the ultimate goal should be its elimination—insofar as that is possible. Some believe, however, that a preoccupation with the total elimination of addiction and with the cure of individual addicts has unnecessarily limited efforts at more general medical management of the addiction problem. Thus it has been widely argued that any treatment program under which some addicts might receive medically prescribed drugs would involve doctors in the perpetuation of disease and amount to an abandonment of the effort to cure addiction. This argument conveniently ignores the fact that addiction is actually being perpetuated under the present arrangements, even if doctors play no direct part in its perpetuation. As the author of the New York Academy of Medicine's 1955 proposal for narcotics clinics pointed out:

> We are not saying to give the addicts more drugs. We are simply advising a different method of distribution . . . every addict gets his drug right now . . . why not let him have his minimum requirements under licensed medical supervision, rather than force him to get it by criminal activities, through criminal channels?[75]

Increasingly, proposals for narcotics reform urge placing as many addicts as possible under some kind of medical management. Treatment should depend on the particular addict's problems and prognosis. If medical administration of drugs is necessary even for a prolonged period—during efforts to enlist cooperation in a cure, or in a case in which cure seems unlikely—then such administration (occurring as part of an over-all treatment program) should be considered a legitimate aspect of medical practice in this area. These proposals involve recognizing that different types of addicts may require varying treatment approaches. Even more significantly, perhaps, they offer a major advantage conspicuously absent from all crash programs to cure individual addicts. Medical administration of low-cost legal drugs could drastically undercut the economic incentives underlying the illicit traffic and could largely eliminate various secondary aspects of addiction as a social problem.

The British Experience

Realization of this possibility has heightened American interest in Great Britain's approach to the narcotics problem.[76] In sharp contrast with American drug policies, the British procedure is to treat addiction almost entirely as a medical matter. The general tenor of public policy was suggested in the 1926 report of a governmental advisory committee: "With few exceptions, addiction to morphine and heroin should be regarded as a manifestation of a morbid state, and not as a mere form of vicious indulgence." [77] Under the Dangerous Drugs Act[78] and supplementary regulations, the British maintain careful control over the possession and supply of opiates (and certain other drugs). Authorized drug-handlers must keep full records of all drug transactions, and such records are subject to periodic inspection by the Home Office and special Ministry of Health inspectors. Doctors who improperly divert narcotics supplies to their own use or who otherwise violate the drug laws are subject to fine or imprisonment, and also may lose the right to possess and prescribe such drugs. The treatment of addicts, however, rests with medical practitioners. Although the government advises doctors to exercise caution in prescribing narcotics, physicians may in fact legally supply narcotics to addicts:

> . . . morphine or heroin may properly be administered to addicts in the following circumstances, namely (a) where patients are under treatment by the gradual withdrawal method with a view to cure, (b) where it has been demonstrated, after a prolonged attempt at cure, that the use of the drug cannot be safely discontinued entirely, on account of the severity of the withdrawal symptoms produced, (c) where it has been similarly demonstrated that the patient, while capable of leading a useful and relatively normal life when a certain minimum dose is regularly administered, becomes incapable of this when the drug is entirely discontinued.[79]

A Home Office memorandum to doctors warns that "the continued supply of drugs . . . solely for the gratification of addiction is not regarded as a medical need," [80] but the physician remains the final arbiter of what constitutes proper medical treatment of addicts. There have been only a few cases in which physicians had been prosecuted for what was thought to be overprescribing to addicts; when there is such a prosecution, the courts tend to uphold the physician's professional judgment. Inspection of drug records is used mainly to uncover doctor-addicts who may prescribe for fictitious patients. Even when such instances come to light, the doctor is likely to receive a relatively light punishment—typically a fine and withdrawal of his authority to possess and prescribe dangerous drugs.

There is no required registration of addicts in Britain, but doc-

tors are requested to inform the Home Office of addicts coming to
their attention and it is believed that the Office's file contains brief
data on most of the country's addicted persons. The British make
no provision for compulsory commitment of addicts, but most doctors apparently do try gradually to reduce the addict's dosage and
to induce him to undergo institutional withdrawal treatment. An
authoritative American report has summarized the British policy as
follows:

> . . . the British medical profession is in full and virtually unchal-
> lenged control of the distribution of drugs, and this includes distribu-
> tion, by prescription or administration, to addicts when necessary.
> The function of the police is to aid and protect medical control,
> rather than to substitute for it.[81]

In 1961, a British governmental study found this policy to be working well. Changes *dis*approved by an Interdepartmental Committee
included compulsory committal, compulsory registration of addicts,
and the establishment of specialized-treatment institutions. It stated
also that "irregularities in prescribing of dangerous drugs are infrequent and would not justify further statutory controls." [82]

Under this policy the British addiction problem has remained
remarkably benign.[83] There are believed to be less than one thousand opiate addicts in the entire United Kingdom. There is practically no illicit traffic in opiates, because the legal provision of
low-cost drugs (the addict qualifies as a patient under the National
Health Service and is charged only two shillings per prescription)
has largely eliminated the profit incentives supporting such traffic.
Similarly, as already noted, serious addict-crime is almost nonex-
istent. The addict in Britain need not become a thief or a prostitute
in order to support his habit. Very few addicts are imprisoned for
any sort of offense. Occasionally an addict will commit a minor
violation of the narcotics laws (for example, forging a prescription)
to increase his legally prescribed dose, but such incidents are not
frequent. Addiction and the underworld have not become inter-
meshed, and there has been no serious spread of narcotic addiction
to juveniles. British policy has also inhibited the development of

an addict subculture. The addict is not subjected to a continuous
struggle for economic survival and for drug supplies, nor need he
constantly attempt to maximize his anonymity and mobility. There
is relatively little need for group support, and actual contact with
other addicts may be slight. Despite the lack of compulsory commitment and special treatment, there is no evidence that the British
have been any less successful in treating addiction as a disease than
we have in this country. It is, in fact, quite possible that a nonpunitive approach, such as the British have taken, increases the
likelihood of enlisting the cooperation of addicts in serious attempts
at cure.[84]

There have been conflicting interpretations of the British experience. The Federal Bureau of Narcotics has sought to convey the impression that British policy is really the same as that in this country
—noting that in Britain narcotics are subject to wide statutory control and that indiscriminate administration of drugs to addicts is
not permitted. Attention is focused on the warning against prescribing "for the mere gratification of addiction," while the stated (even
if nonstatutory) criteria for prescribing, as well as the general spirit
of British policy and its actual administration, are largely ignored.[85]
More serious arguments concern the significance of Great Britain's
successful control of addiction and its relevance to the drug problem in this country. Some observers believe that the British have
been able to adopt a nonpunitive policy precisely because of the
benign nature and extent of their addiction problem. Likewise it
has been suggested that the vastly differing drug situations in the
two countries, as well as more general cultural differences, render
the British experience largely irrelevant to the American situation.[86]

On the other hand, there is no denying that the British have kept
addiction under remarkable control, and it would seem that their
refusal to treat the addict as a criminal has at least helped to keep
him from becoming one. The differences between the two countries
and their addiction problems do not, in themselves, invalidate elements of medical and sociolegal soundness embodied in the British
policies. Clearly, Great Britain has developed no secret formula that
would solve the addiction problem in the United States. And it is
possible that disputes about the British system have even confused

the discussion of proposals for changing American policy. Proponents of a reform cite the British approach with approval—not as a universally applicable panacea, but as an illustration of the common sense and humanity felt to be lacking in American policies, and as evidence that a medically oriented approach to addiction need not have disastrous effects.

Steps Toward Reform

For some years it has been evident that the American medical profession does not entirely support prevailing antinarcotics measures. One of the first major statements by an important medical organization was made in 1955 by a committee of the New York Academy of Medicine:

> There should be a change in attitude toward the addict. He is a sick person, not a criminal. That he may commit criminal acts to maintain his drug supply is recognized; but it is unjust to consider him criminal simply because he uses narcotic drugs. The Academy believes that the most effective way to eradicate drug addiction is to take the profit out of the illicit drug traffic.[87]

To that end, the committee proposed a national network of federally controlled dispensary-clinics at which addicts could receive drugs at low cost. The clinics, it was felt, would provide a setting for intensive treatment efforts and research. In a second report, issued in 1963, the Academy reviewed the controversy caused by its original proposals, evaluated findings and arguments concerning the British experience (from which the committee found "nothing that alters and much that supports its conception of what ought to be done in the United States"), and strongly reaffirmed its earlier call for a medical approach to addiction. The committee emphasized that present policy does nothing to curb illicit traffic by removing profit incentives, and unnecessarily hampers doctors in their treatment of addicts. The report concluded with an insistence that the addict be considered a sick person: "This attitude should be a dominant thesis permeating and setting the tone in the policy and practices of every agency." [88]

Also very influential has been the report of a joint committee of the American Bar Association and the American Medical Association—originally issued in 1956 and published for general distribution in 1961.[89] A comprehensive analysis of the entire drug problem, this report recommended the establishment, on a controlled basis, of an experimental out-patient clinic for the treatment of addicts, in order to explore the possibilities of treatment in the community as well as in institutions. Other medical groups and prominent individuals have urged reforms which would include experimentation with out-patient treatment and even maintenance administration of drugs. The official position of the AMA on these matters now seems to be that although it does not approve of either procedure, limited experimentation on these matters by qualified practitioners is consistent with good medical practice.[90] Such experiments are beginning to be undertaken. The National Association for the Prevention of Addiction to Narcotics (NAPAN) has announced two pilot programs that will test ambulatory treatment,[91] and the New York State Department of Mental Hygiene has begun a small-scale experiment to test the consequences of providing addicts with controlled doses of drugs.[92] The results of these preliminary tests will have to be assessed cautiously. Because different types of addicts may require or be amenable to different forms of treatment, no single path for the future treatment of addiction is likely to be indicated. On the other hand, if the subjects in these experiments have been carefully chosen, and if excessive generalization from the findings is avoided, some new light may be thrown on the diversity of possible treatment approaches.

Such experimentation may be expected to continue for some time, but recent and pending legislation and pronouncements at the 1962 White House Conference on Narcotics and Drug Abuse[93] indicate that the major innovation in narcotics policy in the near future will be the "civil commitment" approach. Under this plan (variants of which have been adopted in New York and California), some addicted narcotics offenders are given the option of undergoing treatment while criminal charges are held in abeyance. Although these plans do envision some possibilities for voluntary commitment, it

appears that they will typically operate after arrest—merely providing an alternative disposition of the offender. The program may
afford certain addicts a little better treatment than they would have
received under previous laws, but the total punitive context would
not be significantly altered. As Lindesmith has stated:

> The system's faults appears to be limited applicability, reliance on
> coercion, failure to make any fundamental change in the structure of
> the criminal law and failure to give the medical profession an im-
> portant role. The plan will probably not materially affect the illicit
> traffic, the criminality of addicts or the spread of the habit.[94]

Such a program seems unlikely to meet with much success, for it
relies on a form of compulsory treatment. Though some proponents
of civil commitment have given the impression that it represents a
real breakthrough toward a medical policy on addiction, critics state
that it is a weak compromise reflecting at best an ambivalence in
the attitude toward the addict.

This ambivalence was seen in the recent report of the President's
Advisory Commission on Narcotics and Drug Abuse.[95] The Commission recognized that harsh legal sanctions will not by themselves
solve the narcotics problem and called for increased emphasis on
rehabilitation. It proposed amendment of existing laws with their
mandatory minimum sentences to allow for more judicial discretion, particularly in cases involving possession of drugs without intent to sell. Although it recommended new treatment programs and
more assistance to treatment efforts, the Commission strongly sup-
ported the civil commitment idea, and in fact called specifically for
a federal civil commitment law. Although the Commission rather
abruptly dismissed the British experience and stated the dominant
view opposing out-patient treatment and the sustaining of repeatedly
relapsing addicts on maintenance doses, it did approve experimentation in these areas, and also called for amendment of the existing
federal regulations on medical treatment of addicts. The Commission also proposed some organizational changes which could have
the effect of more strictly limiting the Bureau of Narcotics' activities to law enforcement matters.

Arguments Against Legalization

Although there is a growing receptiveness in the United States to the redefinition of drug addiction as a medical problem, strong opposition continues to be directed against any plan that can be construed as involving legalization of addiction. One of the key arguments has already been noted—that any legal provision of drugs to addicts constitutes an abandonment of the fight to eradicate addiction. A second line of opposition asserts that legalization would not produce the desired beneficial results. Addicts, it is claimed, would not be content with the legally provided drugs, and illicit traffic and addict-crime would persist.

In this connection, federal drug officials frequently cite the early and largely unsuccessful experiment with municipal drug clinics. Between 1912 and 1925 there were clinics dispensing low-cost narcotics to addicts in over forty American cities. These institutions operated for varying lengths of time and with varying degrees of efficiency and success; eventually they were all closed down by the federal government. There is considerable dispute about this clinic program. Some accounts indicate that in certain localities legal provision of low-cost drugs by the clinics cut significantly into the black market as well as putting large numbers of addicts into contact with medical men. It appears that the clinics were shut down largely on the basis of complaints against the one in New York, which was so badly mismanaged that its activities hardly provided a reasonable basis for any general evaluation of a clinic program.[96] However, it is clear that medical men were disillusioned about the operation of clinics, and in 1924 the American Medical Association passed a resolution calling on federal and state governments "to exert their full powers and authority to put an end to all manner of so-called [i.e., out-patient] ambulatory methods of treatment of narcotic drug addiction, whether practiced by the private physician or by the so-called 'narcotic clinic' or dispensary." At least until very recently this resolution has been cited by the Federal Bureau of Narcotics as constituting the final and unchallenged stand of the medical profession, and as support for the Bureau's opposition to a full medical addiction policy.[97]

It is evident that the clinic experiment was not a striking success, but few impartial experts infer from it the inevitable failure of any such program. A key question, of course, is whether the addict's increasing tolerance will always cause him to seek more and more drugs, and hence to be unsatisfied with legal supplies. There is considerable argument about this point, and (as noted) some experiments designed to discover the answer are now being conducted. It is known that at least some addicts have been able to get along fairly well on relatively stable doses, and the British experience seems to lend further support to this possibility.

It is sometimes argued that medical management of addiction would actually make the situation much worse—in particular, that it would lead to a vast increase in addiction. In suggesting this, opponents of reform have been less than scrupulous in their characterization of reform proposals. They have, for example, described plans for a medical approach as involving "giving everyone free access to drugs." Such characterizations ignore the general treatment context within which any proposed prescription of drugs would occur, as well as the fact that all such plans limit the program to existing addicts. Furthermore, as the New York Academy of Medicine has pointed out, even in those relatively few instances where (after careful clinical evaluation) maintenance is deemed necessary, the cases would be kept under continuous review. Most of these patients would be maintained "only until it was determined that withdrawal was appropriate and they were ready for it. For many the period would be short." [98]

It is true that legal administration of drugs to known addicts would not directly produce any decrease in the number of addiction cases, but that would not be the immediate purpose of such a program. On the other hand, as a careful analysis of the various arguments recently noted: "There is not the slightest reason to suppose that the new policy would increase the number of addicts. If anything, it would tend to inhibit the induction of new cases." [99] This is because, as has already been seen, significant effects on the illicit traffic could be expected.

At the core of much of the officially expressed opposition to drug-law reform has been the conviction that addiction is a vice which should not in any way be condoned and that the addict is basically a wrongdoer and not just a sick person. The Federal Bureau of Narcotics has ignored the fact that addiction is no more condoned by being managed medically than it is by being fostered illegally. It has refused to recognize the element of compulsion underlying the addict's behavior, and the fact that legal pressures account for much of his criminal activity. Representative of this viewpoint is the assertion by former U.S. Commissioner of Narcotics Harry Anslinger that almost all addicts are parasites and that "the parasitic drug addict is a tremendous burden on the community." [100] During his tenure of office, critics stressed the influence of Anslinger's views and activities, often calling for his retirement (which took place in 1962) as a key prerequisite to reform.[101]

Public Attitudes Toward Addicts

Opponents of reform have insisted that public opinion would never countenance a radical change in narcotics policy. According to one law enforcement officer, addiction is similar to robbery in that "both of these types of behavior, even though they were not illegal, would still be offensive to the great majority of the public, which would react by lynch law or some other type of punitive activity." [102] Actually, statements of this sort represent mere assumptions as to how allegedly right-thinking people should or will feel. There are not many data directly bearing on public attitudes toward addicts and addiction. Although a few studies have revealed strongly punitive outlooks on narcotics use, it is likely that these views are now being tempered by the new emphasis on medical approaches. As the public gets more accurate information about addiction, it is more likely to distinguish in its judgments between the addict and the nonaddicted distributor. It has been pointed out, too, that such punitiveness as does exist has been largely the result of the long-time dissemination of antiaddict views by narcotics officials. Public opinion cannot be presented as the basis or justification for a punitive policy when it has—at least in part—been created by that policy.[103]

Various factors may account for the wide public acceptance of punitive attitudes on addiction. Like the homosexual, the addict has long served as a scapegoat:

Addicts, to a greater or lesser extent, always have been a pariah class which has not been in a position to refute any charges levelled against it. Apparently it gives people some kind of secret satisfaction to call names when they cannot understand.[104]

Some of the hostility toward addicts has undoubtedly been due to the misconceptions fostered by the "dope fiend" myth. But even among individuals who reject the myth there may be little sympathy for the addict. The very passivity and unproductiveness characteristic of most addicts are strongly disapproved of in the dynamic, work-oriented American society. The fact that some addicts would work reasonably well when receiving legally prescribed doses might not greatly influence the general reaction, even if it were more widely known. That the acceptance of certain relatively unproductive individuals might be less socially undesirable than the forcing of such individuals into overtly antisocial acts is a viewpoint that has yet to receive wide approval.

Until recently, the addict had few public spokesmen while the repressive, antiaddict attitude received strong support from public officials. Indeed, some critics argued that these officials had developed a vested interest in existing policies. In a sense, the medical profession also benefited from such policies, which relieved the profession of the responsibility for dealing with addiction. Inability to effect easy and lasting cures, and the well-known fact that addicts are extremely difficult patients, may have contributed to medical ambivalence toward drug-law reform. One of the major factors behind such policy changes as are now taking place is the medical profession's apparent willingness to accept increased responsibility for the treatment and management of addicts. Although this change of heart may reflect an acceptance of some of the sociolegal considerations outlined in this chapter, it is more likely caused by an unwillingness any longer to countenance the inhumanity of present policy and by the realization that addicts as "human beings in distress are morally entitled to the best help that can be offered them. . . ." [105]

Summary

In the United States it is not, strictly speaking, a crime to be a drug addict. Yet this is the practical effect of the statutes that make it illegal for the addict to possess the narcotic he craves, and of regulations inhibiting (virtually banning) the prescription of these drugs to addicts by physicians. The addict's consequent illicit purchase of narcotics clearly constitutes a victimless crime as the concept is defined in this book. The addict is unlikely to complain against his illicit provider, and hence the laws banning such transactions are highly unenforceable. As in the case of abortion, a powerful illegal traffic in the demanded commodity arises; here the profit incentives are tremendously heightened by the continuous nature of the addict's demand and by his almost unlimited vulnerability. As in the case of homosexuality, the addict role may often take on primacy, as the entire existence comes to be centered around the need to finance and supply the drug habit.

The effects of this situation, in shaping the addict's self-image and behavior, are profound. The need to counteract law enforcement efforts and to maintain continuous contact with illegal drug sources, together with the enveloping and long-term nature of the shared adjustment problems, lead to the development of a special addict subculture. The problem of drug addiction can be seen, then, as embodying—in perhaps even more extreme form—tendencies observed in the examples of abortion and homosexuality. The unenforceability of the law, the growth of a thriving and well-organized illicit traffic, the secondary deviance on the part of the offending individual, the development of criminal self-images, and the evolution of a large-scale deviant subculture are all present.

In recent years there has been an increasingly strong current of professional opinion asserting that addiction should not be considered a crime at all but, rather, a disease. It is contended that treating the addict as a patient rather than as a criminal might drastically reduce the secondary aspects of the narcotics problem. Reform proposals aimed at undercutting the illicit traffic in drugs and putting most addicts under medical care often include the possibility of medical provision of low-cost drugs where that is deemed necessary. Such plans are still the subject of much controversy, but compromise measures (including greater judicial discretion in sentencing of drug violators, more and better treatment programs, and compulsory civil commitment for treatment) have already been enacted in some jurisdictions. The prospects for more thoroughgoing reform will depend largely on the overall attitudes toward addicts and addiction developed in the concerned professional groups and disseminated to the public at large.

Notes

[1] Alfred R. Lindesmith, " 'Dope Fiend' Mythology," *Journal of Criminal Law and Criminology,* 31 (1940), 199-208.

[2] D. P. Ausubel, *Drug Addiction: Physiological, Psychological and Sociological Aspects* (New York: Random House, 1958), p. 18.

[3] This point has been raised in critical reviews of Jack Gelber's *The Connection* and other plays and novels about addiction, the critic sometimes maintaining that addicts are not interesting subjects for fictional presentation because "they just sit around and don't really do anything."

[4] Isidor Chein, *et al., The Road to H: Narcotics, Delinquency, and Social Policy* (New York: Basic Books, Inc., 1964), p. 356.

[5] Helen M. Hughes (ed.), *The Fantastic Lodge: The Autobiography of a Girl Drug Addict* (Boston: Houghton Mifflin Company, 1961), pp. 113-14.

[6] See Alfred R. Lindesmith, *Opiate Addiction* (Bloomington: Principia Press, 1947).

[7] Hughes, *op. cit.,* pp. 127-28.

[8] Chein, *et al., op. cit.,* pp. 246, 347-48.

[9] Expert Committee on Addiction-Producing Drugs *Seventh Report,* World Health Organization Technical Report Series No. 116, 1957. As reprinted in President's Advisory Commission on Narcotic and Drug Abuse, *Final Report* (Washington, D.C.: USGPO, 1963), p. 101.

[10] New York Academy of Medicine, Committee on Public Health, "Report on Drug Addiction—II," *Bulletin of the New York Academy of Medicine,* 2nd series, 39 (July 1963), 441-42.

[11] See Ausubel, *op. cit.,* p. 23.

[12] Addict quoted by L. Guy Brown, *Social Pathology* (New York: Appleton-Century-Crofts, Inc., 1942), p. 217.

[13] Chein, *et al., op. cit.*, especially pp. 237-50.

[14] For a good summary of the psychiatric approach see Marie Nyswander, *The Drug Addict as a Patient* (New York: Grune & Stratton, Inc., 1956), Chap. 4; also *Drug Addiction: Crime or Disease?* Interim and Final Reports of the Joint Committee of the American Bar Association and the American Medical Association on Narcotic Drugs (Bloomington: Indiana University Press, 1961), pp. 50-59.

[15] See L. Kolb, "Types and Characteristics of Drug Addicts," *Mental Hygiene,* 9 (1925), 300-13.

[16] Alfred R. Lindesmith, "The Drug Addict as Psychopath," *American Sociological Review,* 5 (1940), 920.

[17] Lindesmith, *Opiate Addiction, op. cit.,* p. 69 see also his "A Sociological Theory of Drug Addiction," *American Journal of Sociology,* 43 (1938), 593-613.

[18] Chein, *et al., op. cit.,* p. 24.

[19] Howard S. Becker, *Outsiders: Studies in the Sociology of Deviance* (New York: The Free Press of Glencoe, Inc., 1963), Chaps. 3 and 4.

[20] R. E. L. Faris and H. W. Dunham, *Mental Disorders in Urban Areas* (Chicago: University of Chicago Press, 1939).

[21] John Clausen, "Social Patterns, Personality and Adolescent Drug Use," in A. Leighton, J. Clausen, and R. Wilson (eds.), *Explorations in Social Psychiatry* (New York: Basic Books, Inc., 1957), p. 238.

[22] Chein, *et al., op. cit.,* p. 78.

[23] *Ibid.,* p. 92.

[24] *Ibid.,* p. 187.

[25] *Ibid.,* pp. 268, 273.

[26] John Clausen, "Social and Psychological Factors in Narcotics Addiction," *Law and Contemporary Problems,* 22 (Winter 1957), 34.

[27] New York Academy of Medicine, *op. cit.,* p. 430.

[28] *Webb v. U.S.,* 249 U.S., 96, 100 (1919).

[29] Rufus G. King, "The Narcotics Bureau and the Harrison Act: Jailing the Healers and the Sick," *Yale Law Journal,* 62 (April 1953), 736-49.

[30] *U.S. v. Behrman,* 258 U.S. 280 (1922).

[31] *Linder v. U.S.,* 268 U.S. 5 (1925).

[32] See U.S. Bureau of Narcotics, "Prescribing and Dispensing of Narcotics Under Harrison Narcotic Law," Pamphlet No. 56 (Washington, D.C.: USGPO, 1956).

[33] New York Academy of Medicine, *op. cit.,* p. 432, citing statistics from L. Kolb, *Drug Addiction: A Medical Problem* (Springfield, Ill.: Charles C. Thomas, Publisher, 1962).

[34] *Drug Addiction: Crime or Disease?, op. cit.,* p. 78.

[35] 65 Stat. 767, 21 U.S.C. Sec. 174 (1952).

[36] 70 Stat. 567 (1956).

[37] For a good survey of state laws see Donald J. Cantor, "The Criminal Law and the Narcotics Problem," *Journal of Criminal Law, Criminology and Police Science,* 51 (January-February 1961), 516-19.

[38] State of New Jersey, Executive Department, Assembly Bill No. 488, veto message of Governor Robert B. Meyner (mimeo, June 28, 1956), p. 5.

[39] Vincent Riccio and Bill Slocum, *All the Way Down* (New York: Ballantine Books, Inc., 1962), p. 145.

[40] Robert K. Merton, *Social Theory and Social Structure,* rev. ed. (New York: The Free Press of Glencoe, Inc., 1957), p. 79.

[41] Statement of Lawrence Fleishman, U.S. Customs Bureau, in U.S. Senate, Committee on the Judiciary, Subcommittee to Investigate Juvenile Delinquency. *Hearings*, Part 13. New York City, September 20-21, 1962 (Washington, D.C.: USGPO, 1963), p. 3140.

[42] Malachi L. Harney and J. C. Cross, *The Informer in Law Enforcement* (Springfield, Ill.: Charles C. Thomas, Publisher, 1960), pp. 17-18.

[43] *Sherman v. U.S.*, 356 U.S. 369 (1958), as reprinted in R. C. Donnelly, J. Goldstein and R. D. Schwartz, *Criminal Law* (New York: The Free Press of Glencoe, Inc., 1962), p. 729.

[44] *Rochin v. California*, 342 U.S. 165, 172 (1952).

[45] Robert Alden, " 'Beatnik' Police Seize 96 in Narcotic Raid," *The New York Times*, November 9, 1959, p. 1.

[46] John M. Murtagh and Sara Harris, *Who Live in Shadow* (New York: Ballantine Books, Inc., 1959), p. 99.

[47] See Robert M. Lipsyte, "Cops in the World of 'Junk'," *New York Times Magazine*, October 14, 1962, p. 63 *et seq.*

[48] L. Kolb, "Drug Addiction in its Relation to Crime," *Mental Hygiene*, 9 (1925), 75-76.

[49] Chein, *et al.*, *op. cit.*, pp. 166-67.

[50] Harold Finestone, "Narcotics and Criminality," *Law and Contemporary Problems*, 22 (Winter 1957), 71.

[51] See *ibid.*, p. 82.

[52] Statement of Commissioner Michael J. Murphy, U.S. Senate, Committee on the Judiciary, Subcommittee to Investigate Juvenile Delinquency, *op. cit.*, p. 3080.

[53] Harold Finestone, "Cats, Kicks and Color," *Social Problems*, 5 (July 1957), 3-13.

[54] *Ibid.*, p. 5.

[55] Seymour Fiddle, "The Addict Culture and Movement Into and Out of Hospitals," as reprinted in U.S. Senate, Committee on the Judiciary, Subcommittee to Investigate Juvenile Delinquency, *op. cit.*, p. 3156.

[56] *Ibid.*, pp. 3157-60.

[57] Hughes, *op. cit.*, p. 143.

[58] Fiddle, *op. cit.*, p. 3158.

[59] *Ibid.*, p. 3159.

[60] Chein, *et al.*, *op. cit.*, p. 192.

[61] Charles Winick, "Physician Narcotic Addicts," *Social Problems*, 9 (Fall 1961), 178.

[62] Marsh Ray, "The Cycle of Abstinence and Relapse Among Heroin Addicts," *Social Problems*, 9 (Fall 1961), 132-40.

[63] See Alfred M. Freedman, "Treatment of Drug Addicts in a Community General Hospital," *Comprehensive Psychiatry*, 4 (June 1963), 199.

[64] Ray, *op. cit.*, p. 136.

[65] Freedman, *op. cit.*; also Freedman, *et al.*, "Response of Adult Heroin Addicts to a Total Therapeutic Program," *American Journal of Orthopsychiatry*, 33 (October 1963), 890-99.

[66] Statement of Rev. Norman Eddy, in U.S. Senate, Committee on the Judiciary, Subcommittee to Investigate Juvenile Delinquency, *op. cit.*, p. 3152.

[67] Freedman, *op. cit.*, pp. 205-206.

[68] See Gilbert Geis, "Narcotic Treatment Programs in California." Paper pre-

sented at conference sponsored by Massachusetts Health Research Institute and U.S. Public Health Service, Chatham, Mass., September 1963. Especially pp. 10-15.

[69] Rita Volkman and Donald R. Cressey, "Differential Association and the Rehabilitation of Drug Addicts," *American Journal of Sociology*, 69 (September 1963), 129-42; also Lewis Yablonsky, *The Violent Gang* (New York: The Macmillan Company, 1962), pp. 253-63.

[70] David Sternberg, "Synanon House—A Consideration of its Implications for American Correction," *Journal of Criminal Law, Criminology and Police Science*, 54 (December 1963), 447-55.

[71] Nyswander, *op. cit.*, p. 116.

[72] Hughes, *op. cit.*, pp. 214-15, 232.

[73] Marie Nyswander, *et al.*, "The Treatment of Drug Addicts as Voluntary Outpatients: A Progress Report," *American Journal of Orthopsychiatry*, 28 (October 1958), 704-27.

[74] Thomas Szasz, *Law, Liberty and Psychiatry* (New York: The Macmillan Company, 1964); Erving Goffman, *Asylums* (Garden City, N.Y.: Doubleday & Company, Inc., 1961).

[75] Hubert S. Howe, testimony, U.S. Senate, Committee on the Judiciary, Subcommittee on Improvements in the Federal Criminal Code, 84th Cong. 1st Sess., *Hearings,* Part 5 (September 1955), p. 1332.

[76] For a more detailed discussion of this approach, see Edwin M. Schur, *Narcotic Addiction in Britain and America: The Impact of Public Policy* (Bloomington: Indiana University Press, 1962); "British Narcotics Policies," *Journal of Criminal Law, Criminology and Police Science*, 51 (March- April 1961), 619-29; "Drug Addiction Under British Policy," *Social Problems*, 9 (Fall 1961), 156-66. See also Alfred R. Lindesmith, "The British System of Narcotics Control," *Law and Contemporary Problems*, 22 (Winter 1957), 138-54; and Rufus King, in *Drug Addiction: Crime or Disease?, op. cit.*, pp. 126-39.

[77] Ministry of Health, Departmental Committee on Morphine and Heroin Addiction. *Report* (London: His Majesty's Stationery Office, 1926), p. 31.

[78] 14 and 15 Geo. 6, Ch. 48 (1951). This act consolidates all previous narcotics legislation, which began with the original Dangerous Drugs Act in 1920.

[79] Ministry of Health, *op. cit.*, p. 19.

[80] Home Office, "The Duties of Doctors and Dentists Under the Dangerous Drugs Act and Regulations," 6th ed. D. D. 101 (London; Her Majesty's Stationery Office, 1956), p. 2.

[81] King, in *Drug Addiction: Crime or Disease?, op. cit.*, p. 127.

[82] Ministry of Health, Interdepartmental Committee on Drug Addiction, *Report* (London; Her Majesty's Stationery Office, 1961).

[83] Schur, *Narcotic Addiction in Britain and America . . . ,op. cit.*

[84] Edwin M. Schur, "Treatment Implications of British Narcotics Policy." Paper presented at annual meeting of American Orthopsychiatric Association, Los Angeles, March 1962.

[85] Advisory Committee to the Federal Bureau of Narcotics, "The British System" (mimeo, July 3, 1958). See also G. W. Larimore and H. Brill, "The British Narcotic System: Report of Study," *New York Journal of Medicine,* 60 (1960), 107-15.

[86] Larimore and Brill, *op. cit.*

[87] New York Academy of Medicine, Committee on Public Health, "Report on

Drug Addiction," *Bulletin of the New York Academy of Medicine*, 31 (1955), 592.

[88] New York Academy of Medicine, Committee on Public Health, "Report on Drug Addiction—II," *op. cit.*, pp. 467, 468.

[89] *Drug Addiction: Crime or Disease?, op. cit.*

[90] See President's Advisory Commission, *op. cit.*, Appendix.

[91] See *NAPAN Newsletter* (October 1963), 1.

[92] Thomas Buckley, "State Giving Narcotics to Addicts in Test," *The New York Times*, March 9, 1964, p. 1.

[93] Proceedings of the White House Conference on Narcotic and Drug Abuse (Washington, D.C.: USGPO, 1962).

[94] Alfred R. Lindesmith, "Addiction: Beginnings of Wisdom," *The Nation*, January 19, 1963, 49.

[95] President's Advisory Commission, *op. cit.*

[96] Nyswander, *The Drug Addict as a Patient, op. cit.*, p. 8.

[97] See Federal Bureau of Narcotics, "Prescribing and Dispensing of Narcotics Under Harrison Narcotic Law," *op. cit.*, p. 8.

[98] New York Academy of Medicine, "Report on Drug Addiction—II," *op. cit.*, p. 451.

[99] Chein, *et al., op. cit.*, p. 376.

[100] H. J. Anslinger and W. F. Tompkins, *The Traffic in Narcotics* (New York: Funk & Wagnalls Co., 1953), p. 170. For a more recent statement of Anslinger's views see H. J. Anslinger and Will Oursler, *The Murderers* (New York: Farrar, Straus & Company, 1961).

[101] See, for example, Murtagh and Harris, *op. cit.*

[102] Arthur M. Grennan, "The Policeman's Viewpoint," in William C. Bier (ed.), *Problems in Addiction* (New York: Fordham University Press, 1962), p. 199.

[103] Edwin M. Schur, "Attitudes Toward Addicts: Some General Observations and Comparative Findings," *American Journal of Orthopsychiatry*, 34 (January 1964), 80-90.

[104] Lindesmith, "The Drug Addict as a Psychopath," *op. cit.*, p. 919.

[105] Chein, *et al., op. cit.*, p. 380.

Crimes Without Victims

The Concept

Now that several crimes without victims have been examined in some detail, it may be useful to consider more generally the meaning and significance of that phrase. It refers essentially to the willing exchange, among adults, of strongly demanded but legally proscribed goods or services. Do prohibitions of this sort, and the social problems to which they are directed (and of which they are a part), constitute a sociologically meaningful category? H. L. A. Hart has asked: "Ought immorality as such to be a crime?" [1] Crimes without victims involve attempts to legislate morality for its own sake; the two conceptions very largely relate to the same thing. From the sociological standpoint, however, reference to the victimless nature of the offense may have certain advantages. It reveals the basis for saying that certain laws are indeed designed merely to legislate morality. It also highlights an important criterion for determining which laws fall into this category—the question: "Is there, in this particular situation, any real victimization?"

Another concept closely related to the analysis in this book is *dissensus*. With respect to each of the cases examined here, there is a lack of public consensus about the law. However, consensus is similarly lacking in the enactment and execution of other criminal laws, yet not all those instances involve the peculiar characteristics of the deviance situations described here. For instance, not only is there extensive violation of existing income tax laws, but there also appears to be considerable ambivalence in public attitudes toward these statutes (at least toward their specific provisions if not their very existence). But although these laws are not easily or completely

169

enforceable, they do not give rise to the secondary elaboration of deviance and the related problems evident in the examples discussed above. A main point of differentiation seems to be *the element of transaction, or exchange.* Crimes without victims may be limited to those situations in which one person obtains from another, in a fairly direct exchange, a commodity or personal service which is socially disapproved and legally proscribed.

This limitation is admittedly somewhat arbitrary. It can be seen that there are other offenses in which there really is no victim. And if one were solely concerned with straight description, the phrase *exchange crimes* or even *business crimes* (i.e., offenses giving rise to illegal businesses) might be almost as appropriate a label for the subject matter of this book. But, as already mentioned, the concept of victimless crime helps to pinpoint a major criterion for evaluating policies, and this, too, is of concern in this discussion. The limitation of the concept to the exchange situations keeps it from getting out of hand. In a sense, every criminal law represents a societal judgment establishing both an offender and an individual or collective victim. Where there is direct offense by one person against another person or his property, the victim and victimizer are easily identified. On the other hand, in a crime against the state or a crime against morals, the victim becomes more elusive. And when the law specifically insists that a person is a victim even if the facts contradict that contention—for instance, sexual intercourse with a girl "under the age of consent" is statutory rape, even though she consents—the victim element is blurred still further.

In the examples considered here, the "harm" seen in the proscribed transaction seems primarily to be *harm to the participating individuals themselves* (apart from any alleged harm to general morals). Does the term *self-harm,* then, adequately describe the situations being considered? Not quite. In the first place, there is much dispute as to the extent of self-harm actually involved in the various proscribed behaviors. But, beyond that, not all proscriptions of self-harm produce situations of the sort analyzed here. Thus legal attempts to ban suicide or masturbation might seem to establish victimless crime situations in the sense of prohibiting self-harm, but precisely because the offense involves only the lone individual there is little or no basis for any elaboration of the deviance. Perhaps it is *the combination of an exchange transaction and lack of apparent harm* to others that constitutes the core of the victimless crime situation as here defined. Not all "exchange crimes" would qualify, because in some there may be evident harm to others. This is seen in the case of wartime black-market operations, in which the exchange of proscribed but strongly demanded goods between willing sellers and buyers does work patently to the disadvantage of many other individuals. Perhaps it is because the buyer of such goods is attempting to get more than his fair share of commodities desired by a large proportion of the general citizenry that dispassionate observers can easily view his behavior as harmful to society.[2] Of course it must be kept in mind that even dispassionate analysts will differ in their assessments of the harm involved in particular situations, and indeed there will be some individuals who see distinct harm to others even in the nonvictim situations described in this book.

One feature which seems to characterize all crimes without victims is the unenforceability of the laws surrounding them. Such *unenforceability stems directly from the lack of a complainant* and the consequent difficulty in obtaining evidence. Also significant is the low visibility of these offenses. If for some reason the proscribed exchanges had to occur always in public, enforcement would be far more efficient. Obviously the willing nature of the interpersonal exchange and the privacy in which it can take place are related. Another apparent consequence of privacy and lack of a complainant (combined with public ambivalence about the law) is the invitation to police corruption. Outside of these points, however, there is considerable variation within the category of crimes without victims. A comparison of the three situations analyzed in this book, may provide some hints as to the factors determining the expansion of deviance in the victimless crime sphere.

The Self-Image

In all three cases, the individuals involved tend to develop, in some degree, a deviant self-image. This is largely the result of the dominant social definition of their behavior as being outside the pale of respectability, and the more specific labeling of the behavior as "criminal" reinforces and heightens this process. It is, of course, very difficult if not impossible to draw a clear-cut distinction between a deviant self-image and a criminal one. In a sense perhaps only differences of degree exist. Yet the criminalization of deviance may have an especially crucial influence on the individual's view of himself. Thus, the realization that they are considered criminals and —even more significantly—the need to act like criminals causes most drug addicts in this country to develop—at the very least—a pronouncedly antisocial outlook. The doctor-addict, though also clearly a deviant, is unlikely to consider himself a criminal because he can maintain his habit with relative ease and through quasilegal means. The extent of deviant self-image seems, then, to be directly related to the degree of primacy[3] taken on by the deviant role, or the extent to which the deviant behavior comes to be elaborated into a role at all. And primacy relates closely to the *extent to which the deviant must, in order to satisfy the proscribed demand, engage himself in various instrumental and supportive activities.*

The Subculture

This raises the matter of subculture, the development of which is similarly dependent on the nature and extent of the engagement or involvement required of the particular type of deviant. There is pronounced subcultural development in the cases of homosexuality and drug addiction but none in the case of abortion. (Quite simply, in getting what she is looking for, the woman who has had an abortion has no need for frequent or continuing contact with other abortion-seekers.) Partly, it would seem, the development of a subculture has something to do with the continuing nature of the deviant behavior. Generally speaking, abortion is a discrete act, which one can easily bracket in time and space. This explanation is too simple, however, for the physician-addict is indeed continuously addicted yet he does not display subcultural involvement. It is not then merely the continuing nature of the basic deviant act that establishes the basis for a subculture but, again, the *need for continuous contact with other like individuals in order for the basic deviant acts to be carried out.* (There are, of course, psychological considerations which—as noted in the specific studies—may well exert some pressure on deviants to come together, even in the absence of practical need.) This assertion still leaves open the question of how and to what extent legal repression affects such need. Earlier chapters have suggested some instances of fairly specific and direct influence. Perhaps the best example is drug addiction, where it seems clear that the curbing of legitimate supplies tremendously increases the addict's practical need for involvement with other addicts. The role of law in stimulating the development of deviant subculture is less clear in the case of homosexuality. It is interesting to speculate, for example, that the homosexual subculture would be appreciably weaker if all confirmed homosexuals were free to embark on homosexual marriages without fear of legal interference. As noted in the introduction, it is extremely difficult, in trying to answer such questions, to analyze the effects of legal sanctions apart from the influence of the concurrently existing general social disapproval.

It should be clear from this discussion that deviant self-images and involvement in deviant subcultures are interrelated phenomena. Involvement in such a subculture, however, is not an absolute prerequisite to the development of a deviant self-concept. The physician-addict, for example, may well have a consciousness of his continuing deviance and experience great uneasiness about it, even if he has not become generally alienated and totally self-condemning. Likewise, engagement in deviant or criminal behavior may have a pronounced impact on one's self-concept even when the individual is not involved in continuous behavior patterns that imply taking on a set and deviant role. The guilt feelings of the aborted woman serve to illustrate such possibilities.

Secondary Crime

A consideration of the development of an illicit traffic reveals further variation among the three victimless crimes. In the case of abortion and drug addiction, there is a thriving illicit market, although the degree of elaboration and organization may be somewhat greater in the drug situation—owing perhaps to the continuous and particularly compulsive nature of the addict's demand. A related point may be that the addict demands a scarce commodity, whereas the abortion-seeker requires a personal service. It may be somewhat more difficult to supply the commodity, and possibly this may intensify the profit factor and thereby strengthen the black-market operation. However, it should be stressed that the *demand for services as well as that for goods can indeed provide the basis for illicit traffic.* Not only is this seen in the abortion situation, but also in the somewhat analogous cases of prostitution and gambling (which would seem to be two more major examples of victimless crime). Perhaps the most interesting point of variation regarding illicit traffic is its very slight development in connection with homosexuality. As already noted, this appears to be owing to the peculiar supply-demand situation regarding such deviance; the homosexual need not (and, in fact, may only infrequently) turn to nonhomosexuals to effect the proscribed transaction.

It may also be useful to consider why the drug addict engages in much secondary crime while the deviants in the other two situations do not. Obviously the immediate cause is the financial pressure the addict faces in attempting to support his habit. To what, in turn, may this be attributed? Again, the fact that the addict seeks a commodity might seem relevant, although this factor does not appear to be conclusive. Rather it is *the continuous need for what the illicit market has to offer, together with the fact that such offering must be paid for,* that drives the deviant into secondary crime. It is quite possible that a woman continuously seeking abortions could come under severe financial pressure and resort to crime to finance such activity. But most women do not seek abortions continuously, and so the problem does not arise (though in the lower socioeconomic strata some petty crime to finance even a single abortion may occur). Among compulsive gamblers, where there may be almost no limit to the funds the individual requires in order to engage in the desired activity, financial pressures can easily lead to secondary crime.

The Social Reaction

The analysis of abortion, homosexuality, and drug addiction also illustrates some general aspects of social reaction to deviance. In all three cases, public reaction and existing legislation are at least partly based on vital misconceptions about the nature of the deviant behavior. This is not, of course, an inevitable characteristic of public reaction to all deviance, nor is there something about the victimless crime situation that necessarily implies such misinformation. And it should be stressed that stereotyped notions certainly are not the sole support of existing reactions to these problems. Still, the prevalence of misleading notions is startling, and it is particularly interesting that in all three cases *information about relatively harmless aspects of the deviance has not received wide attention.* Thus the real effects of opiates on the addict's behavior and physical condition, the relative safety of most hospital abortions, and the nonstereotypical behavior of many homosexuals—all key facts—have been insufficiently emphasized in popular discussions of these forms of deviance. This can be attributed, in part, to mere lack of information; at the same time, it seems apparent that opponents of reform proposals have made it a point to neglect such factors—which would, after all, considerably weaken their arguments.

This suggests the importance of the group and individual functions or interests served by existing policies, which—as suggested in Chapter 1—may extend far beyond the obvious economic interests of illicit suppliers. Such functions vary considerably in nature and intensity. There is, for example, the rather specific and strong vested interest of a specialized law enforcement agency, such as the Federal Bureau of Narcotics. Or there may be a less direct group interest served. Thus, with regard to both addiction and abortion, present policy may in some measure reflect the medical profession's ambivalent attitude toward taking on major responsibility for management of the problem. On the individual level, punitive reactions to deviance may serve various kinds of functions. Every deviant is, in some sense, a psychological scapegoat—a social sacrifice who complements and at the same time establishes the very possibility of conformity in other group members. The special characteristics of any one form of deviance help to determine the ease or difficulty with which it can provide (at a particular time and in a particular society) a basis for such sacrifice.

In light of these considerations, it is interesting that usually the professed aim of legislation against deviance is to eliminate the offending behavior. In the case of drug addiction, for instance, the exclusive emphasis on complete cure of individual cases and on total elimination of addiction has hindered treatment experimentation and other policy reforms. In all three problem areas, the actual effect of the policies employed has been to regulate, and not to eliminate. Despite pious protestations, it seems clear that *the repressive policies discussed in this book represent societal decisions as to how the various demanded goods and services are to be allocated.* Embodied in these decisions is an insistence that social approval shall not attach to the transactions in question; but also implied is the recognition that the particular goods and services shall in one way or another be made available. The woman is to be relieved of her unwanted pregnancy, even if reputable hospitals are not to cooperate. The drug addict is to obtain his drugs, but not from legitimate medical sources. The homosexual is to pursue his sexual inclinations, but must conceal his condition and submit to a certain amount of segregation. Of course very few citizens in our society would express the collective decisions in this way. Yet one is forced to conclude that for one reason or another it has been "arranged" that these social problems shall remain insoluble. Perhaps there is much that is sociologically, as well as psychologically, suggestive in the question posed by Paul Reiwald: "Is the contention exaggerated, or does it not rather state the simple truth, that man has contrived his institutions for the combat of crime so that he may in fact maintain it?" [4]

Policy Reform

What, if any, are the over-all policy implications to be derived from this discussion of crimes without victims? I have certainly not meant to suggest that all "difficult" criminal laws ought be abolished forthwith. At the same time I have indeed tried to indicate the importance of examining the operation and impact of such laws, rather than simply accepting them as given and therefore valid. Furthermore, it must be clear that if one is to draw any policy conclusions at all in areas of this sort, ultimately a personal value judgment must be made. The discussion has, in each of the three areas examined, outlined some of the apparent consequences (or concomitants) of present policy and speculated on those which might attend alternative policies. Even such a presentation must go somewhat beyond available empirical findings. But in any case, individual evaluation of the picture presented will inevitably depend on subjective factors. In attempting to compare alternative sets of social gains and costs (which is what must be done in reaching any sound policy decision), different individuals are likely to assign different weights to particular constituent elements of the problem, and they will also differ in their assessments of the final balance of gains and costs. For this reason there is simply no way to prove scientifically the "best" policy regarding any one type of deviant behavior. What can be done—and, hopefully, what has been done—in this book is to provide a broad picture of the total problem (and of the likely alternatives), on the basis of which individuals can decide what policies to advocate and support. There are also many specific issues relating to the particular deviance situations on which further intensive research (not attempted here) will help fill in major gaps in current knowledge.

Legalization is not automatically or invariably to be preferred to criminalization. Actually the term *legalization* has been used primarily by opponents of reform, to create misleading impressions of reform proposals. For one thing, supporters of existing policies sometimes picture any one proposal for change in criminal law as part of an ominous and general trend toward the legalization of all deviance. Yet there is no general policy principle to be applied to all types of deviance. Each particular type displays its own peculiar characteristics and raises its own special problems which must be considered for policy purposes. There has also been a tendency to use the word *legalization*—with its handy connotation of *no* restriction—to exaggerate specific recommendations for reform of particular deviance policies. It has been alleged that reformers would "allow everyone free access to dope," or would permit "complete license in sexual behavior," or "let any woman wanting an abortion get one." Actual proposals for policy change are almost never so extreme. Similarly, suggestions that legalization implies moral approval or at least condonation are misleading. Liberalization of a law on deviance may imply less disapproval than currently exists, but less disapproval is not the same as positive approval. And at least from a sociological standpoint, concentration on the moral evaluation of the deviant behavior—viewed in the abstract—is hardly profitable. The more constructive sociological task is to try to understand the behavior in its relation to human needs and social values and institutions, and to help decision-makers determine which policy will best maximize social gains and minimize social costs.

An important consideration that may influence acceptance of specific policy changes has to do with the means by which the good or service might be legally provided under a nonrepressive policy.[5] In the case of abortion and addiction, the medical profession would replace the illicit operatives as suppliers of the demanded goods and services. In the case of homosexuality, no such currently legitimate source of supply would be involved. Because no "outside" group would have to be implicated in dealing with homosexuality (i.e., all that would be required would be to allow these people to conduct their own relationships without interference), in a sense reform of these laws might seem easier than in the other two examples. This difference may more likely, however, have just the opposite effect. It may be that medical provision in the abortion and addiction situations provides a basis for legitimation of the transaction not possible in the homosexuality case. (Such grounds for legitimation would be similarly lacking in the case of prostitution—where short of converting prostitution into a respectable profession there seems to be no way of altering the aura under which the services are provided.) Legitimation through medical auspices suggests the significant point that increasingly, in analyses of deviant behavior, the discussion has centered on the issue of whether the behavior in question should be considered a crime or an illness.[6] Even sociologists who would be quite unwilling to accept the proposition that all deviants in these borderline areas are sick may see a tactical need to accept the definition of illness in order to achieve humanitarian and common-sense reforms. Until the public is able to acknowledge that more subtle and sociological forms of determinism are generating and shaping deviance, this strategem will continue to be employed even in cases where it may be inappropriate.

There is, then, an urgent need for increased public education and wider appreciation of sociological perspectives on deviance. It is often maintained that public opinion will not countenance increased permissiveness toward deviant behavior. Yet, as has already been pointed out, knowledge of such opinion is actually quite limited. Furthermore, whatever opinion does exist has often been shaped by misinformation and by the very punitive policies in question. Fortunately much of this misinformation is now being brought out in the open and refuted. This is important because only as the more conforming individuals in society attempt to understand the motivations and patterns of deviance[7] can we hope to grapple effectively and sanely with what is, after all, an unavoidable aspect of social life.

Notes

[1] H. L. A. Hart, *Law, Liberty and Morality* (Stanford: Stanford University Press, 1963), p. 4.

[2] I am grateful to David Matza for suggesting this point and the general relevance of the black market example.

[3] See Edwin Lemert, *Social Pathology* (New York: McGraw-Hill Book Company, Inc., 1951), especially Chap. 4.

[4] Paul Reiwald, *Society and its Criminals,* translated by T. E. James (London: William Heinemann, Limited, 1949), p. 173.

[5] I am indebted to Peter Gens for suggesting the importance of this factor.

[6] See Thomas Szasz, *Law, Liberty, and Psychiatry* (New York: The Macmillan Company, 1963), especially Chaps. 2 and 3: and Erving Goffman, "The Medical Model and Mental Hospitalization," in *Asylums* (Garden City, N.Y.: Doubleday & Company, Inc., 1961), pp. 323-86.

[7] See Howard S. Becker (ed.), *The Other Side: Perspectives on Deviance* (New York: The Free Press of Glencoe, Inc., 1964).